To Peggy & Clayt —
my Two best friends!
(I didn't think all that easy)
Charlie Brower

# ME, AND OTHER ADVERTISING GENIUSES

# Me, and Other Advertising Geniuses

## Charlie Brower

DOUBLEDAY & COMPANY, INC.
GARDEN CITY, NEW YORK 1974

ISBN: 0-385-02469-X
LIBRARY OF CONGRESS CATALOG CARD NUMBER 73–83617
Copyright © 1974 by Charles Brower
All Rights Reserved
Printed in the United States of America
First Edition

To Betty, my wife


With deep gratitude
to Ed Roberts, who wanted
to get *all* the facts and
stories together, and
died trying.

ME, AND OTHER ADVERTISING GENIUSES

# Intro

☞ I shall never forget those days in advertising kindergarten when we sat in our little red chairs and sang our class song:

*Tell me quick*
*And tell me true*
*Or else, my love,*
*To Hell with you!*

We not only learned to write the Lord's Prayer on the head of a pin, but on the point! The reader of advertising must *never* be bored, and if we couldn't be bright we could at least be brief.

Consequently, I can now write a whole book on a single sheet of paper. The trouble is, no one but me would know it was a book. Others would think it was just a sheet of paper.

A thin book, they tell me, is 60,000 words. I do not think there *are* 60,000 words, even if you include those that were once unus-

1

able. But I was never one to shirk a job just because it made no sense. How else would I have been able to live for forty plus years in this wonderful, painful, frustrating, exuberant, rewarding, depressing and exciting business?

And look, Mom, no ulcers.

Judge Oliver Wendell Holmes said, "A man must feel the passion and action of his time, on peril of being judged never to have lived." The Advertising Business is where it's at, Judge.

# Shambling
# briskly

---

# 1

☞ Reactions were mixed along what we laughingly call Mad Av when the news broke that I was to be president of BBDO. Some sniggered. Some laughed out loud. Some paled. Some threw up.

Clients quaked like aspen leaves . . . who is this guy? . . . where did *he* come from? . . . dunno, dug him up somewhere. . . .

The eight-million-dollar Revlon account that had been teetering on the tenth-floor window ledge, while dozens of anxious advertising agencies waited below with nets, finally jumped.

So what is he going to do about that?!

Not knowing the answer, I said we would go out and bring in eight new accounts of a million dollars each. We did somewhat better than that three years later, being awarded Pepsi and Dodge, but I didn't know it then.

Bill Burding of Lever Brothers phoned to say that he had wanted to kick us out for months—but he didn't know who to talk to. Now that I was in, they were out. Others were obviously looking around—in advertisingese it is called "reviewing our advertising setup." But few survive the review.

Alex Osborn, a name on the door, said he would like to be called a "friend of the management," not part of it.

The press was kind. *Fortune* gave me a double column. *Business Week* put me on one of their covers. *Time* magazine traced my long and bumpy history. The *Wall Street Journal* gave me several lines on their front page.

Years later I heard a rumor (untrue, I believe) that other members of the Executive Committee had agreed that—should anything happen to Ben Duffy (and something was *always* happening to Ben)—I would not be allowed to inherit the throne.

I would gladly have signed such an agreement. Who wants a fifty-six-year-old president who weighs in at 220, stands six feet four, walks as though bucking a strong wind, is gifted with incurable sarcasm, doesn't know a single headwaiter and doesn't even have his own table at "21"?

Besides, I didn't want the job at all. I had served my time—thirty years—and had gone through all the lower chairs from trade and industrial copywriter to Executive Vice-President in Charge of Creative Departments. I didn't really need the money. I had earned retirement.

But all of us reckoned without my wife, who knows nothing much about advertising, but quite a lot about me. When I made these General Sherman disavowals to her, she said: "Pardon me, but isn't that your tongue I see hanging out?" I looked and bygod she was right.

I decided to make a run for the roses. First, I had to create a new image. For the first time in my whole life, I tried to look and act the part of an adman. I got modest clothes and drowned some of my more snarling neckties. I tried to walk briskly even if I was only going to the men's room. I put a curb bit on my sarcasm. And I smiled like a political candidate.

It was a brief act, and a dramatic flop. It is impossible to shamble (*Time* mag) briskly. My sarcasm had little to do with me. It seemed to act independently of wish or thought. So I told a writer who showed me an idea that had struck him "like a bolt

*4*

from the blue," "George, it looks to me as though you'd been struck by a broomstraw."

I was sarcastic at age four. An elderly cadaverous female asked, "What are you going to be when you grow up?"

I answered, "A man!" (leaving unspoken, "you stupid old crow"). Suddenly I was snatched to her bony bosom and covered with dried up kisses.

"That's the *greatest* thing *anyone* can *ever* be," she croaked. "A real man. Your mother should be proud of you."

Right there is when I should have joined Smart Asses Anonymous. But alas, I didn't, and my number of friends has shrunken to those who "understand" my disease.

My attempts at smiling were even more disastrous. People who once turned pale at my frown, fainted dead away at my smile. They thought I was baring my teeth at them.

I went back to being my old abnormal self. It made everyone more comfortable. People started coming out of the woodwork and urging me to run. "Fine, I *am* running, pass it along." Someone sent me a picture of a wedge of ducks flying, with an arrow in ink pointing to the lead duck. Caption: "Please be our leader." All very sweet, but the working folk do not elect the president in our company. The Board of Directors does, and they usually follow the lead of their Executive Committee.

I went to see each director, except two, who might consider themselves candidates, urged on by Jim Schule, the Board's secretary, and later executive vice-president.

The day before the directors meeting, I walked into Jim's office.

"I do not want anyone embarrassed tomorrow," I said, "so I would like you to tell every director who is opposed to me that I will be elected."

"What makes you think so?" asked Jim, who knew everything that went on around the place—a male Mother Superior.

"How about nineteen sure votes?"

"Exactly how I had it figured. Congratulations!"

And so I was elected, with a few grumpy absentees.

My own reaction was not pride. It was fright. I knew no more about management than I did about Mars. I never considered my years as head of creative departments as "Management." It seemed to me to be much more like a lion tamer's job . . . win the trust of the cats, be their friends, have no favorites, don't give them too much raw meat, and *never* turn your back.

Jim tried to throw some calm over my worries.

"This agency has so much going for it that even *you* couldn't kill it in ten years."

But people had reason to be worried. They knew that I was no Ben Duffy. He oozed Irish charisma, and everybody oozed right back at him. He hadn't just kissed the Blarney stone, he carried it with him. He was a natural people-lover. In important places, we were known as "Ben Duffy's Agency." And no doubt we still would be, had he not suffered a crippling stroke.

I worked out a simple philosophy—so simple that I could understand it myself. It went like this: Reward the truly great people a lot better, try to move the just average people into the great-people classification. Fire those who will not develop their skills or have none, no matter if some are your best friends. In brief, fewer and better people, more highly paid.

For people in advertising death rides a taxicab. We are forever saying, "What if so-and-so got struck by a taxi?" Nobody ever has, except one came close, and was killed by a police prowl car. To face such dire possibilities, we carry, or used to, "Key Man Insurance." My importance can be measured by the fact that my policy (payable to the company) was for $5,000.

Alex Osborn (now a friend of the management) thought it ought to be raised to $100,000.

"If anything happens to me," I said, "a hundred thousand dollars won't help things much."

"What about your salary? Shouldn't it be raised to, say, sixty thousand dollars?"

"Alex," I said, "either I am going to be good at this job, or not. I want my salary left just where it is until we all decide that I am doing a good job. Then my salary is going to have to be considerably higher than sixty thousand."

I was getting a bit cocky for me. Maybe the rat race wasn't so bad if you were the head rat. Then John Redmond Kelly hit the fan.

6

Channing Pollock pointed out that every generation has some members that insist upon attacking Gibraltar with peashooters.

Away back in 1925 Earnest Elmo Calkins wrote to another ad man: "You are probably aware, as I am, of the large number of criticisms being hurled at advertising from all sources. I have counted eight destructive articles in the last two months. I have promised to prepare a sober and well considered article for the *Atlantic Monthly,* stating where advertising stands today, in which I plan to take up some of the more popular criticisms of advertising and dispose of them."

# Who killed
# poor John?

## 2

☞ The one paper that gave me the full treatment, no longer exists, nor does its editor and publisher. It was about the size of Gallagher's fountain of truth, but frankly printed on yellow. An agency man has to read these things, because his clients do. The yellow sheet was called *Quest* and its entire staff, as far as anyone knew, was John Redmond Kelly. Its masthead promised cheerfully that it was a weekly. Most people figured it came out every time John Redmond Kelly repossessed his typewriter.

Did he give me space! The whole front page and a good bit of the acreage inside. Even today it makes nice reading.

### WILL BBDO TEAR OUT BIG BEN'S HEIR?

BBDO's Boney Prince Charlie's coronet is ill-fitting and more often than not askew. It cannot be determined finally

9

at this point whether the coronet is too big, or Charlie's head is too small. It can be stated with justification, however, that Charlie Brower's recent intermittent eccentric performance is a classic case of square peg in round hole. Some days the coronet slips over Brower's eyes. Blinded and befuddled he stumbles and trips in the dark, with alarming and disconcerting results. By the time Brower has adjusted his headpiece Charlie Revson has trucked his bottles and banana oil out of Zeckendorf's juke-box lobby and into the street. Still in a state of scotomatic shock, Charlie Brower goes "Poo, Poo" and predicts that it will be replaced in a matter of hours with eight $1 million accounts. A statement like this leaves many old-timers at the top and intermediate levels of BBDO in a state of confusion. They wonder "Is Charlie making private jokes?" They wish he would explain them or desist. They sigh "If Ben were only here." They complain about Charlie's sarcasm, his wise cracks. They are looking in vain for that promised eight one-million dollar accounts. They feel they need a fence mender and Brower does not fill the bill. They worry about his tendency to wave a big stick at clients. They feel that NOBODY is that big. Uneasy lies the head that wears a crown, and in its present uncertain position it could slip down far enough to strangle the agency.

Naturally, my joy at being thus praised was less than infinite. I decided to ignore him. There is that old advice about never getting into a pissing contest with a skunk. So I made no reply to Mr. Kelly's infrequent bouts of advice and turned toward better literature. Then he went too far. He referred to Tom Dillon, then treasurer and now president of BBDO as "Snuffy Smith"! That was too much.

My clients, bless them all, insisted that I do something about Kelly. They figured that by not answering him I was admitting the truth of what he said. And they, as clients, felt implicated in my shame.

But how? Could I run ads in the trade books saying that I was not a stupid idiot? Or a befuddled bum? Not after many years of advising clients not to reply to unjust attacks. This only calls attention to the original attack, and brings it to the notice of many who have not heard of it before.

Again I called for help from Jim Schule, who, among many other jobs, ran our legal department. He was also a Knight of Malta, and a Knight of the Holy Sepulcher.

There was only one thing wrong with Jim. He went to Mass every day of the year. I told him he ought to cut down a bit on this frequency of exposure, or somebody up above might tip off St. Peter, who would send for him to help straighten out heaven, just as he was straightening out BBDO. I was right, too. They nabbed him a few years ago. Age, fifty.

"How," I asked Jim, "in this land of free speech, can you shut a man up, just because you do not like what he is saying about you?"

"If what he says about you is not true," Jim replied, "you have a good slander case. I think you could win it. About ten years from now we might come to trial. You would win, and get all he has, his old typewriter."

"Thanks a lot. You're a real pal!"

"Maybe you could steal his typewriter!"

"Oh, great!"

"We could send him a case of scotch every week. Then he wouldn't be able to write!"

"Stop kidding, this is getting to be a great big problem."

"You've got bigger things to worry about. Forget it and I'll think of something."

I did not see any more copies of *Quest*, but a few weeks later John Redmond Kelly made the real newspapers. He had been found dead in the basement of his apartment house, apparently murdered.

"Jeez, Jim," I said to Schule, "I didn't want you to go *that* far!"

"It's nothing to joke about! I sinned once by wishing him dead!"

"I was only kidding!"

"It's not very funny!"

Who did kill John Redmond Kelly? I do not know, nor have I worried much about him. What I worried about was who, in BBDO, had been leaking our troubles to him.

During my advertising career, there have been three self-appointed gadflies, buzzing and stinging around the ad business. One was *Space and Time*, which was innocuous and infrequent. Then Kelly. And now Bernie Gallagher. He started after me, too —although in a somewhat more gentlemanly manner, mostly by calling attention to our mistakes (we made them *then*) and playing down anything good we might have done.

I took him to lunch and found that he was a professional Irishman, sore because he thought we had shortchanged another Irishman, Ben Duffy. I suggested that he call Ben and find out what he was talking about. Ben (as I have been) was treated royally.

He apparently was satisfied—maybe too satisfied, because he started calling me "Four-Square Charlie" in his sheet, which did come out on a regular schedule, and painting me so lily-white I could hardly recognize myself. I asked him to cut that out, too —people might think we were engaged.

Many people dislike Gallagher. And "dislike" is a nice word for how some feel. But I was never able to work up such a dislike. Gallagher was, and I presume still is, one of the world's truly great fiction writers.

During our last declared war, advertising was signally honored by being placed just ahead of "Artificial Flower Manufacturers" on the United States Government's list of non-essential industries.

---

General Electric began to receive letters, chiefly from New England, asking if "the bright star that shines in the Western sky was placed there as a memorial to Thomas A. Edison."

GE's press bureau issued a statement: "This myth has existed for some years in the minds of a good many people. Some have asked: 'I should like to know what the Edison Star is made of, what causes the light, and the object of doing so.' Others wanted to know how many miles of cable were required to supply the star with power and supposed it took a good many."

This is probably the best publicity that Venus ever got until the Russians started sending probes there.

# The man
# everybody
# knew

## 3

☞ Unlike Alex Osborn, who wanted only to be a "Friend of the Management," Bruce Barton wanted very much to help. The main trouble with Bruce was that he was very old—the same age that I am now. It is said that there are only two kinds of men and women—those born with two drinks in them, and those born needing two drinks. Bruce was born with two drinks in him, but occasionally he needed a little addition. Our disastrous trip to Minneapolis was one of them. I probably knew more clients in Minneapolis than he did, but he was going to introduce the new BBDO president if it killed him, which it may have.

It was Sunday around noon when I met him at Kennedy Airport.

"First of all," he said, "I need a drink!"

In New York bars open on Sunday at 1 P.M.—the exact time of

our flight. I should have foreseen this, but I hadn't, so I said cheerfully, "The minute we get aboard, we'll have a double."

I rang for the hostess and told her that we were somewhat desperate. Could she do us a great favor and take care of the situation now, before we took off?

"We serve no drinks until after lunch," she said.

"I think you must be a little confused," I said. "Cocktails are served before meals. In fifty states they serve them before meals. On the ground, on the sea and in the air, cocktails are served before meals. And on this plane they are supposed to be served before meals."

But nothing shook her resolution. She must have been a dropout from Hostess School like another I met once, who refused to give me a second scotch. Scotch, she figured, was dangerous stuff. If I had wanted a second drink, I should have ordered martinis like everyone else. And that's the way it was. First the meal, then cocktails, which we no longer wanted.

In Minneapolis, I might better have introduced Bruce. Except for Harry Zinsmaster, a local baker, who had been a classmate of Bruce's at Amherst, Bruce did not really know anyone.

Bruce wrote a great piece once, "Who Knew Not Joseph." Its story line was that Joseph was practically the number two man in Egypt until a new king arose who knew him not. The moral was: "Know Everybody." If you don't you may find yourself facing a stranger one day who would rather have someone else help him rule.

At the height of his career, Bruce did know everybody, and everybody knew him. He gave great speeches and wrote great books. You might not consider *The Man Nobody Knows* or *The Book Nobody Knows* to be great books. But they were best sellers in their time, and Bruce might have been a truly great man, except for a small prejudice against too much work and too many hours.

Kids who wanted to write, stopped him on the street with questions.

"Do you write from inspiration, Mr. Barton?"

"You bet I do. Every time Esther, that's my wife, says, 'Bruce, just look at that rug. It has a hole all the way through it,' I get inspired to write enough to buy a new rug."

"What would you advise a young man to do?"

"Go down to Wilmington and marry one of the Du Pont girls. There are *millions* of them."

But by 1957 most of the people he was going to introduce me to were no longer around. I went to a party he gave at his home on Fifty-fifth Street, and my wife and I, then in our middle fifties, were treated like kids by the happy oldsters. It had been many years since I was rated as "not dry behind the ears yet." It was a farewell party, given by Bruce for himself because he was going to Italy next day. He taxied to the ship, then wondered, "Why the hell am I going to Italy?" and finding no answer, stayed in the taxi and drove back home.

Bruce's talks to introduce me to Minneapolis were mostly about himself, and his friends and escapades of long ago. I followed nervously, and tried to explain my plans for the agency, which had not quite jelled. We did not go over very big. One small man in a client's advertising department said we would have done better to stay home.

On the second day of our planned three-day stay in Minneapolis, we were invited to go afloat on Lake Minnetonka in a public relations man's nightmare probably dreamed up by us. That year's Minnesota Dairy Queen was to cruise about in a barge just like Cleopatra, except that Cleopatra probably did not have a cow aboard, as well as a couple of crates full of PR men. The cow had done something unusual—not with the moon but with butterfat.

The queen, who looked as though she were carved of ivory, and thought that way, too—had no more than nineteen years on her speedometer. She was seated beside a female PR girl of fifty plus.

Bruce flopped into the nearest available seat, but I thought I ought to greet the queen. Looking at her and the wrinkled one, I asked, "Which of you is the Dairy Queen?" I had intended this for a small forgivable bit of foolishness that might please the elderly PR girl. But it didn't work out that way because the little queen jumped to her feet and insisted loudly that "I AM!" Everyone hated me for making a fool of two women at the same time, and for treating their sacred cow expedition so lightly.

You could have baked a loaf of Zinsmaster's bread on the waters of Lake Minnetonka. Everyone was soaked with sweat except the queen, who had been instructed not to sweat.

The motor purred on. Bruce was clinging to an upright desperately, although the boat did not rock, and he was seated. No one spoke but the cow, who occasionally stopped chewing long enough to emit a booming bawl that could have been heard back home, no matter where she came from.

"I'll bet fifty dollars I can milk that cow!" I could have, too, but I didn't have my white tie and gloves. A few people looked as though they were considering throwing me overboard.

Bruce tottered back to the car an hour later, looking tired and beat. Everyone was ready for a bath and a cooling beverage. Everyone but Bruce, who remained seated, staring straight ahead. Nobody could get him to leave the car for almost half an hour.

I decided that maybe a bit of bullying would work.

"God Dammit, Bruce, if you don't get out of this car, I'll drag you out!"

He got out inch by inch, muttering, "That's the trouble with general managers, they always want to generally manage!" (I had been general manager before I was made president.) Bruce didn't want any dinner. He didn't want anything to drink. He just wanted to go to bed.

We helped him to his room and left him, foolishly accepting his assurances that he would be all right.

Late that night I was awakened by a couple of bellboys who said, "Something must be wrong with your friend." They pointed to a small river of water running from under his door. We unlocked the door. Bruce was sprawled naked across the bathroom floor, his broken dentures scattered about.

We turned off the water—only "HOT" was on and it was overflowing the tub. We dried him off, put him back in bed. Since he was snoring smoothly and it was three o'clock in the morning, we decided not to call a doctor until daylight.

Bruce had awakened during the night and, finding that his ankles were swelling, decided to soak them in the tub. Being half asleep and worn out from the cow cruise—he turned on only the hot water. Then he sat on a small stool and stuck his feet into this scalding water. He jerked his feet up, fell backward and knocked himself out when his head hit the wall behind him.

The next morning he seemed all right, just terribly tired. I dressed him with no trouble, although it isn't easy to tie a bow tie on someone else unless you are married to him. We got him on a plane accompanied by a strong young account executive from Minneapolis. I had another day of client meetings and could not go with him. We called New York, asked that his doctor be notified and a car meet him.

The diagnosis was plain exhaustion from working too hard. All he needed was about a week's rest right there in the hospital. While resting he had a stroke.

Bruce recovered from this stroke and came out of the hospital with no obvious impairment of any kind, except that he looked much older and walked with the uncertain step of a very old man.

Soon he was back in the office every day, accompanied by a nurse. He told his secretary, Louise MacLeod, that he had to take things easier now that he was seventy.

"You are seventy-one," she said. "You were unconscious when you were seventy!"

"My God!" said Bruce. "They don't count *that*, do they?" Bruce lived alone. His wife, Esther, had died first. Bruce had put all his money in her name, because everyone knows that women live longer than men. Then he had to pay a large inheritance tax on his own money. Next, his daughter Betsy drowned, her wheelchair in the bottom of the swimming pool. Then Bruce, Junior, died. Only one son, Randy, survived Bruce, and he only for a few years.

Bruce had two Norwegian maids who took care of him and the house. He told us about it.

"When I wake up in the morning, I don't hop out of bed, rush into the bathroom, take a cold shower or any of that stuff. I just ring and one of the maids brings me breakfast and a copy of the New York *Times*. After I finish my breakfast, I leaf through the *Times*. First I read the front page news, then the advertising column. Then I turn very slowly to the obituary column and—if my name isn't there—I get up and go to work."

As it turned out, he would not have had to go beyond the front-page news. Bruce was not the kind of guy anybody puts in the back of a paper.

Whether he achieved his fondest wish or not I do not know. "When the government opens up my safe-deposit box," he hoped, "they will find a twenty-five-dollar War Bond and a note that says 'Dear Government, Please kiss my ass. Bruce Barton.'"

The law traces its history back to Moses, and Medicine to Hippocrates. Compared to the life and noble service of these much older callings, advertising is an infant. Our faults of taste, quality, and even integrity are many. Yet I console myself with the thought that, if we pour out our pleas to the many in order to influence the few, so does the church. If our failures sometimes seem more numerous than our successes, so are those of book publishers and the theater. If we sometimes influence men to live beyond their means so, sometimes does matrimony. And if we are too often dull, repetitious, and redundant, so is the United States Senate.

Bruce Barton

# California—
# the state
# without
# a future

## 4

☞ The October 26, 1962, issue of *Time* magazine devoted itself to advertising. Twelve "Leaders" were pictured on the foldout cover, brief biographies were printed inside. Of those twelve, only one is still a "Leader." In my bio I referred to myself as from "a long line of New Jersey peasants." This did not please some of my relatives. Even worse, I turned out to be wrong. A DAR-type cousin with a sense of humor, if you can imagine *that*, wrote about our mutual ancestor Tobias Hendrickson, now buried at Yellow Meeting House, where they have church once a year. Tobias was not only in the Revolution, he was an officer! He weighed in at 350 pounds, got aboard his horse with a ladder, and was given an honorable discharge because his appetite was starving the rest of the Army.

I countered that argument, and maybe won, by referring to our great-uncle "Gib," a farmer who had never become addicted to toilet paper. On his deathbed he demanded that the hospital furnish him with corncobs. And thus he died, happy and well scraped.

I had more immediate ancestors. They were called "Mama" and "Papa" and spent all of their lives sewing up holes in their poverty pocket. At the age of two, I tired of Asbury Park, and took off for California. My parents went, too. I had blond curls down to my shoulders, a junior Hippy, and any female who could catch me, running up and down the aisles of the train, would smooch me all over.

We moved to Pasadena, following a disastrous year on a northern ranch that was no ranch at all, just cut-over timberland. Good old Papa had bought it cheap without ever seeing it. In Pasadena we lived on the wrong side of all the tracks, on a lot the shape of Connecticut when, by Royal Grant, it ran all the way to the Pacific. It became "the ranch," to the understandable dismay of the six neighbors that abutted our property. It seemed that we had to have a rooster to keep the hens company, but his clarion crow brought up more than just the sun. Our two cows were always bellowing, either mourning for a past calf or yearning for another. A cow in heat can melt a bullet at twenty paces. Mama explained that the cow had a friend and wanted to visit him. All I knew was that occasionally a man would come and lead old Bess away, and she always returned with a smile on her face.

Papa's job in Pasadena was to sell Industrial Insurance to the underprivileged, mostly Mexicans. It was really burial insurance and Papa had to make the rounds, collecting a dime or maybe even a quarter, each week. At the end of the day, he tied the lines around the dashboard and went to sleep. The horse would bring him home. Then he had to eat, and enter every dime in his route book.

While working on his book, he smoked nickel cigars and sent great belches of acrid smoke through the screens that sometimes brought a timid knock and a query: "Is everything all right in there?" I did not like him very much, because he was always trying to bridge the generation gap with a stick.

My mother was the one I liked, because she was the only person I knew who thought I was smart. Our Sunday School class was the worst that ever infested a church. Mrs. Waterhouse, our unfortunate teacher, told Mama that "Charles was her only comfort."

Dear Old Mother, bless her long-gone heart, said, "You keep your eye on that kid. He is thinking up things for the others to do."

Nobody is really poor if everyone else is poor. The big thing was to stay off relief. People helped by the Associated Charities were untouchables. There was plenty to do—beside milking the cows and having two paper routes. I played a mandolin in the Sunday School orchestra . . . "Work for the night is coming" and such dismal dirges of religion.

I was a member of the Loyal Temperance Legion, where we promised not to

> Buy, drink, sell or give
> Alcoholic liquor while I live
> From all tobacco I'll abstain
> And never take God's name in vain.

I have kept one part of that pledge. As far as I know, I have never given away any liquor.

Sunday was the day I wore shoes. Saturday I spent at the Brookside pool. Other days I attended the Columbia Grammar School, ruled over by Mr. Hill with two feet of garden hose.

When California passed a law banning the whipping and beating of schoolchildren, Mr. Hill announced that he had studied the law carefully and it would not prevent him from kicking us.

I had the pleasure of seeing him cut to ribbons by a dropout who had taken up professional boxing. The dropout was smoking a cigarette. Hill crossed the diamond and said, "Put out that cigarette or leave the grounds!" The dropout replied calmly, "Let's see you make me, you fat hayseed." Even the little girls applauded. I do not remember ever seeing Mr. Hill again.

California, at that time, was thought to be ideal for people who had "consumption." They coughed their way West, bringing remnants of their trade with them. Mr. Neuman, who coughed next door to us, had been a tailor, and he kept me in clothes for quite a while. They never fit, and Mama made the alterations. In appearance I was somewhere between Beau Brummel and a sack of potatoes.

In school you learned things that can be taught by rote. Outside was where you learned about life. My buddy, Kenny, had a morning paper route next to mine. He also had a customer who would not pay up. Easy! I'll fix that! So I stood on the sidewalk at 5 A.M. and bellowed, "This is where Old Lady Tibbets lives, and she won't pay her *Examiner* bill!"

It worked, all right. Mrs. Tibbets paid up. I got fired and had a heart-to-heart talk with the sheriff at his request. What he meant, in advertising language, was that "hard sell" offends "soft sell" people. He also told me that he never wanted to see me again. I didn't want to see him again either. I decided to run away since summer vacation was about to start. Kenny was all for the idea.

I told my mother, of course, and she gave me several Mason jars full of Lincoln pennies. She had failed in her efforts to corner the market. She should have saved Indian pennies. My jars amounted to almost twenty-five dollars. Kenny and I rode our bikes north and joined the Fruit Tramps. They were mostly Okies, although Steinbeck hadn't named them yet. They said "you-uns" and "we-uns" and never dreamed that one day they would be called migrant workers and become a large political issue.

We settled down in an unfurnished room in Dinuba. No chair. No bed. No nothing. But you sleep pretty well when you are sixteen and have spent the day lifting your end of a 300-pound sweatbox full of dried apricots, and dumping it into a grader.

We hadn't figured on a slack period between crops. I finally got down to seventeen cents, the exact cost of a movie. Fifteen cents plus two cents War Tax. There was only one movie theater in Dinuba, the Airdrome. Outdoors, but you couldn't bring your car or horse inside. A player piano mechanized the songs of the time, "Somewhere in France," "My Buddy," "Laddie in Khaki" ("I'm Praying for you"), "Long Long Trail." It was a very sentimental war.

Next morning I got up at dawn and started out to see if I could find some kind of work. I found a great field of watermelons being harvested. The owner was Mr. Watanabe, and he made it very difficult for me to dislike Japanese, even when I was supposed to. He not only gave me a job, but loaned me a dollar and said, "Go get some breakfast first."

I was part of a long line that passed watermelons out to the dusty little road, where they were loaded on trucks. Ahead of us scampered little fellows who cut the stems and stood the melons on end. I got twenty-five cents an hour. They got a dollar an hour, because they were specialists. They could tell at a glance which melons were ripe. They had no time for thumping or sniffing. A glance, a snick of the knife, and they were already looking for the next ripe melon.

I had no desire to become an expert watermelon picker, but obviously I ought to become a specialist at something. First, I would have to finish high school. That meant going home, where Papa would start crossing the generation gap all over. I had developed a rather impressive set of muscles (whatever became of *them?*) and suspected I could take the stick away from him. Mama wrote that they had no money again, shut-off notices were coming in from the gas and electric companies, and I might have to get a job instead of going back to high school.

At just that very time Great Uncle Gib (the corncob man) died. Intestate, of course, but even then we had inherited a fortune: $2,500. Papa, ever the genius, had decided that California would never amount to much anyway. My mother said she had been homesick for New Jersey every day of every year she spent in California. I sure wasn't homesick for it, and even now it seems an improbable place to cause homesickness. We packed enough food for five days in a "telescope," really just a large fiber box, and took off.

As a junior at Pasadena High, I had been one of about three thousand pupils. At Freehold, New Jersey, I was one of three hundred. Also I was the only new face in years. And from California, too! I was elected secretary of the senior class, played center on the football team, and acted in the senior play. I played the part of a limp-wristed English suitor and our teacher thought smoking a cigarette might help register nonchalance. She hooked me, and for forty-five years I smoked like Vesuvius. Only five years ago I kicked the habit. A doctor scared me into it.

Meanwhile, dear old Dad spent what remained of the family fortune on *another* spread of stumps. Even though I had given a ringing speech at commencement on "Why I Will Never Leave the Farm," I still remembered the watermelon pickers and my decision to specialize. Somehow I had to get to college.

My mother died that summer, because she had a fool for a doctor. That ended my interest in the immediate family. I was not going to try growing corn between stumps. I cleared out, became a farmhand at thirty-five dollars a week and reviewed all my high school courses at night.

A year of this, I figured, and I could compete for a scholarship. There were two to a county. And the money was available only to those who intended to study agriculture. I would do something about that agriculture stuff after I won the scholarship, if I did.

I did—a scholarship to Rutgers—and when I gave the joyful news to Aunt Lib (my mother's sister) she burst into tears, begged me not to go and threatened to do it on her knees.

College, she said, was right on the main highway to Hell. Aunt Lib was fifty years ahead of her time!

The gentleman who owned Burma Shave, and advertised it in road signs in series, came in to see us. He wanted to expand his advertising a bit, and asked us to see if he couldn't buy the upper corners of right-hand pages so that he could, in effect, put his sequential road signs into magazines.

Today he might have gotten a nibble or two, but the magazines were riding high then, and only giggled faintly at the idea. He then asked us for our suggestions, but nothing we produced pleased him.

He wrote his own ad which explained how he discovered Burma Shave. He was trying to make a truly outstanding mayonnaise, only to discover that you couldn't eat it but you could shave with it.

---

If "early to rise" is such a big deal, why are all the sweaty people on the 6:15, and all the bankers on the 9:34?

# Aladdin's commutation ticket

## 5

☞ Once in college, I never had time to go to hell, as predicted by Aunt Lib. A lot of time was spent peeking through a dish-return slot to see if a current girl friend was in the dining room with someone else. I did not want her to know that I was a pearl diver, washing dishes for my dinner.

Another large hunk of time was spent in keeping my contract with the Devil, who, that season, was posing as a physics professor. He needed a good mechanic, and I was one until I got married. Also physics was one subject I could transfer to, and thus escape agriculture. The Devil offered me fifty cents an hour. I agreed to major in physics. It was shortly obvious to both of us that I was no threat to Einstein. But the professor needed me, and I needed the job. Without ever discussing it, we agreed that "C" was about as high as you could mark a man who ought to be flunked. By junior year the class was down to five double-domes and me. I could only sit there with my jaw hanging while they discussed "Electron Theory."

My astronomy professor (as a physics major, I had to take that, too) had more fun with me than he could have had with his own rubber duck. He never failed to call on me first. This meant ten minutes of fumbling around for me, and ten minutes rest for him. When he got ready to start the real work, he would rise, yawn and stretch, and say in his impeccable Southernese, "Wall, Mistah Browah, Ah spose ya realize yore no genius!" The class would then laugh politely and I would sit down.

Having saved a bit of money along the way, I decided to hell with this, and switched to nothing but English courses in my senior year. To everyone's amazement I was graduated. I even won the big twenty-five-dollar prize for my work on Eugene O'Neill. I got a Bachelor of Science degree majoring in English. I believe that record still stands.

What does an English major do? Unless he is better heeled than I was, his best bet is teaching. So I had to do practice teaching, too . . . at the Middlesex County Vocational School. These kids were tough and their interest in English literature was as low as their interest in making me miserable was high.

At that time a spelunker named Floyd Collins was making headlines because he had got himself wedged deep in a Kentucky cave where no one could reach him. Every morning the headlines said "Still Alive" and I would say to myself: "If that poor bastard can stay alive in that dark wet cave, I can go one more day to the vocational school."

I snapped up the first teaching job I was offered. It was from Bound Brook, N.J., High School. All I had to do was teach a couple of freshman classes, have all the boys in the high school for physical training, and coach basketball, a game I had never played and seldom watched. The salary, $1,700, would not support a hungry frog. But I had a plan. I would be such an excellent teacher that they would pay me a lot more the following year, maybe $3,000.

The only thing I had to do was to attend the Rutgers Summer Session and take Physical Training, morning, noon and night. I still remember a couple of nuns in full regalia, doing endless push-ups, their beads clacking against the gym floor.

In order to avoid hard work, I was working harder than ever. But at least I was not caddying for cows.

As a matter of fact the school year went very well. I turned out to be a pretty good teacher, and the veteran basketball players taught me how to coach. We even won the county championship.

Came spring and with it the new contract that contained all my hopes. It seems that the Board of Education had been having a bad year. There were only a few raises being given out. One was mine. In one midget leap, I had gone from $1,700 all the way up to $1,750! I never returned the contract. I have it right now in my top bureau drawer, along with fifteen old cigarette lighters, several watches, a handful of gold tees, some broken pencils—the usual top drawer stuff. Now and then I take the contract out and glare at it until it bursts into flame. I never went back to Bound Brook either, except by mistake.

Having $312 and no chance of getting more—I was supposed to be supporting my father, who had no money, either—I was forced to think for the first time in my life. I took inventory of myself to see if there was anything on the shelves that I might peddle to somebody. There was one tiny package: writing. And that was just college stuff. Pretty good considering that we had fewer words available than they do today. Still: college stuff.

Could I write a book? That was sure starvation. Get a job with a newspaper? The big hit in movies that year was *Front Page*, which seemed to prove that newspapermen died of alcoholism at thirty-five. Advertising? It had just become respectable. The signs "No Beggars, Peddlers or Advertising Agents" had all come down. The day when a man said to his wife, "Buy No More from Arnold Constable, they have gone in for advertising," had gone. The word "Hucksters" had no advertising meaning. And the concept of "Hidden Persuaders" would have brought a belly laugh. Unfortunately for me, the advertising agency business was very small and most of the hiring was being done from Yale, Harvard and Princeton—at that time well-known colleges. Knocking on doors got me nothing but distant echoes.

From other job hunters I heard that an advertising big shot was going to give a course in advertising copy at the Columbia Summer School. I decided to roll my shrinking dice in his direction. I would give it plenty of sweat, too. I would be best in show, I *had* to be. Then the agency president, or whoever he was, would say: "You are just the lad I have been seeking. Come and join my agency at a huge salary."

I commuted from an empty fraternity house at Rutgers with a sixty-trip ticket I inherited from a home-bound roommate. It was not just a ticket. It was Aladdin's lamp, if one knew how to use it. Every time the conductor punched it, you looked around the floor for the little pip that had been punched out, replaced it in its hole and glued it in with spit. This worked fine until one day the ticket turned into confetti right in the conductor's hand.

"I guess this ticket is about used up," he said, and I could do nothing but agree.

After that I moved into another empty fraternity house, at Columbia. The decorations were sparce, consisting mostly of a news item pinned to the wall, "Butler Hangs Self." Nicholas Murray Butler was then president of Columbia—and this was a bit of Columbian wit.

Everything worked out as planned. Every day my copy was read out as the best, and the whole class hated me. There were lots of flies that summer, and one was in the ointment. Although the prof liked my work, he never seemed to get around to making that so-essential offer. In desperation, as the term approached its end, I stayed after class and asked him how about it. He agreed that I was a good copywriter and should have little or no trouble getting a job. As for him, he was no big shot at all —just a copy editor at the George Batten Company. But Bill Orchard, who became my close friend and remained so for the rest of his life, was tapped in on the agency grapevine and let me know when a job was opening up.

He set up interviews with Batten people, but none of them seemed to find me irresistible. Maybe it was because my year in Bound Brook had made me look like a schoolteacher. More than likely it was my advanced age. I was twenty-six and the Batten Company preferred them younger. A few years later some of these men were working for me . . . still insisting that they were right not to hire me. "Look what happened!" they said.

The only other agency I tried was J. Walter Thompson. They had an application blank as big as a quilt—based, I think, on Dr. Watson and Behaviorism. I took one look at it and decided I would rather starve.

Macy's advertised for a "Copy Cub" at eighteen dollars a week. But Mr. Goode, who interviewed me, could see through me as though my head were glass.

"You don't really want to work here for eighteen dollars a week. What you want is to get some good newspaper proofs. Then you'll put them in a proof book, get a good job, and quit here."

By this time I had eaten up all my resources and half of my fingernails. I clawed my way through the New York *Times* "Men Wanted" pages and ended up in Boston as a trainee adjuster for a casualty insurance company.

This job consisted in tramping all over Boston in freezing weather, trying to knock down claims of thirty dollars or less. In the afternoon, we would dictate the results of our morning's work, then listen to lectures from the older adjusters.

"Always carry a thousand dollars with you," one of them said, shaking his wad of tens and twenties at us. "You never know when you may be at the scene of an accident. If you are—and one party in the accident is insured with us—you may be able to settle right on the spot at much less than it would cost the company later." With the money I was toting around, I couldn't have settled the damages on a scratched kiddie-car.

Fortunately for me, and the misguided company who thought they could make a claim adjuster out of me, Bill Orchard phoned that there was a job open as assistant advertising manager at Pacific Mills. This was a job he was sure that even I could get.

Bill had some trouble finding me because I was in Peterborough Hospital with a classic case of the mumps. Students from Tufts Medical School visited me almost every day. They brought tape measures, and when they measured they said "wow." They were not measuring my cheeks or jaws either.

One day, having demonstrated my ability to totter slowly across the ward, I was told that I would be discharged when I paid my bill.

"We had better settle down to a long happy life together, if I can't leave until I pay. I think I have two dollars and some change. Is the bill bigger than that?"

They let me sign a note, which they never expected to be paid, but it did get paid eventually. I tottered all the way back to the casualty insurance company. They took one look at me and said, "You're fired!" I didn't bother to remind them that their physician had diagnosed my mumps as "infected salivary glands," and sent me back into the snow. I just said, "I only came back here to quit. You don't have to fire me!"

Bill Orchard got his pal to hold the job open. After two weeks of fattening up at the home of good friends in New Brunswick, and borrowing money from other friends, I went to work.

My eye was still set on the George Batten Company, and something like eighteen months later, Bill Benton cut a hole in the fence and let me squeak through. At last, a chance to show my real talent as a copywriter—the job at Pacific Mills was mostly calling on wholesalers, and writing such headlines as "A Simple Sum in Added Profits."

Unfortunately (I seem to use that word a lot) when I reported for work on the agreed Monday, Benton had been fired for leading some peasant revolt. He says it was for urging a merger with BDO, which took place four months later, and I have never doubted Bill. But he had left in a hurry, and there was no record, written or oral, that he had hired me. Nobody put up a fight when I moved myself into a sawed-off office behind the cashier's cage. This time, if I starved, I was going to make people watch me do it.

Apparently I was successful in driving everyone out of his mind, for, after about three weeks of this, the man who had succeeded Bill Benton as head of the T and I (Trade and Industrial) Department came around and asked me what salary Bill and I had agreed upon.

Some say it was immoral, some say it was slick, but I say I deserved some recompense for the two years I had been kicked around and rejected. So I gave myself a small raise. Even then, it seems that it was not enough. We had a treasurer, born in Kentucky and weaned on Bourbon, who looked almost exactly like W. C. Fields. When he was a schoolboy, living near Lexington, it was not too difficult to get to Churchill Downs at Louisville. It was rumored, and never denied, that in 1902 he sold his school books and put fifty dollars on the nose of Alan-a-Dale, the winner, and came home with money sprouting out of every pocket.

He deserves a chapter, and will get it later. Right now it is enough to say that he came shuffling into my tiny office and asked, "How much would it cost us to get you to move out of that goddam YMCA?"

Frankly, I was shocked. The "Y" had everything a man could desire—a room at four dollars a week (and I got the lower half of the two-story bed)—a swimming pool—bowling—and dancing (with girls).

I figured I could get a room somewhere if I was raised to seventy-five dollars a week. I moved into a one-room-with-bath on Thirty-ninth Street above the Bombay Bicycle Club, a middle-class speakeasy.

Instead of swimming, bowling and dancing I had cockroaches. They would get drunk downstairs and then stagger up to see me. The one distinction this apartment had was a urinal in addition to the other standard equipment. When I was giving a lavish party (applejack and gingerale) and found one of the girls cracking ice in it, I gave up and moved to Bronxville.

That raise to seventy-five dollars a week was the last one I got for years. But that was no problem at the time. I had a friend whose wife was writing scripts for radio. She couldn't handle five a week, so I helped her out with two a week—at a hundred dollars a script. It was a fifteen-minute show—much like "The French Chef," except in our show the vegetables talked. If you have never listened to a really indignant carrot, you probably never will.

The show was called "The Canny Cook" because it was sponsored by a can company. Wit was plentiful in those days. So was optimism. Rose-colored glasses were popular, without bifocals, of course, for nobody wanted to look too closely at anything. Everyone knew that 1928 would be followed by 1929. But no one ever guessed what 1929 was to bring.

One of our favorite girls before she became one of Y&R's favorite girls, accompanied Ray Rubicam on a new business solicitation.

Ray was explaining how short the public memory is, and why it is therefore necessary to keep up a strong and vigorous advertising campaign.

He reminded them that there had been an attempt to assassinate Franklin Delano Roosevelt a few years back. Indeed Anton Cermak, mayor of Chicago had been killed.

And yet Mr. Rubicam felt sure that no one present could recall the assassin's name.

"That's *easy*," said our favorite girl, "his name was Zangara!"

# Benton
# and Bates
# and Bowles
# and stuff

*6*

☞ The Batten Company may have been in a prize-winning building—but the floor-and-a-half in which we lived was out of this world in the wrong direction. Everything was glass from the waist up. Even the window offices had glass fronts. Thus could the gods, and Mr. Johns, see everywhere. The tiny island offices contained exactly one desk, one seat for the inhabitant and another should someone wish to visit him (on visiting day), one typewriter, one coatrack and one fan. With the arrival of air conditioning the fan was no longer needed, so we made the cells still smaller. They were known collectively to their inhabitants as "The Ant Palace."

Oops, I forgot! In one man's tiny office, there was a polo mallet, for prestige purposes.

The coming of air conditioning brought minor tragedy into the lives of the younger male set. The Roosevelt Hotel across Forty-sixth Street put in window boxes, and thus made it impossible to see into the rooms. At its height, room watching occupied an important part of the day. The boys knew all the room numbers *from the outside,* and surprised numerous occupants with phone calls of varying decency.

Jim Nash, a talented package designer, who refused to be fired some years later because he was too busy, was reported to have somewhat hampered a well-developed love scene by phoning, "This is God. Aren't you ashamed?" It didn't bring down the house, but it brought down the window shade. With the coming of window boxes, the lads sadly turned back their creative imaginations to what they were being paid for.

The real *big* men at Batten's . . . those getting between $6,000 and $7,500 . . . were above such childish play. They felt like great men, acted like great men and dressed like great men. It amounted almost to a uniform—a conservative suit, modest necktie, Homburg hat, shoes ever agleam, topped by gray spats. They also wore canes. You did not carry a cane, you wore it.

Most of these top characters subscribed to a flower service. Each morning a dewy carnation or gardenia waited patiently atop your desk, so you shouldn't have to go around all day with a naked buttonhole. Bill Benton said the gardenias were worn by his group of young protesters, and I am not about to deny it. So well dressed were these men that one of them, Charlie Babcock, had a wardrobe in his office. At least one art director first entered the portals of the Batten Company a tailor's errand boy, carrying one of Charlie's eleven suits. If Charlie could see what's being worn these days he'd go back to being dead.

Ted Bates (Yes, Virginia, there *was* one when I started writing this) was a copywriter on Schrader Valves. These were little cores that screwed into tire valves to hold in the air. But when the Continental Baking Company became a client Ted didn't take long figuring out a better future there, and he became an account executive—probably starting on the dream that ended up with Ted Bates, Inc. Ted always ate alone, or with a client, or with a friend named Gildersleeve. Our treasurer—the one who looked like W. C. Fields—sometimes accompanied him to the racetrack, where they had a mutual friend named "The Dancer," who did what parimutuel machines now do. He took your money and occasionally returned a bit of it. Robley Feland, our treasurer, called Ted "Cracked Ice Bates." When Ted got married, I sent him a wedding present. When I got married he sent his congratulations. Johnny Johns, son of our president and a loyal Princeton man, had a standing bet with Bates each year on the Princeton-Yale football game, Bates being a Yaley. This went on for years, Yale always winning handily, making Bates ten dollars richer. Came a season, however, when Yale had few seniors back, and a rather rickety team. Princeton was a powerhouse.

"This year I'll get some of my money back," Johns crowed.

"This year, there'll be no bet," said Bates. "What do you take me for, an idiot?"

Ted worked hard, a rather unfashionable attitude at that time and in that agency. Then, exhausted, and the color of a seasick Chinaman, he would take off for Cuba and return all refreshed again. When he was made vice-president, those of us who worked closely with him gave him a large golden cardboard key labeled "Key to Pee." But it didn't fit. Turned out that the little private toilet on the tenth floor was more private than we knew. It was for directors of the company, not mere vice-presidents. I thought the whole idea was stupidly snotty and said so where it could do me the most harm. The explanation was that it gave the non-directors more freedom. They never had to worry about who might be listening behind those closed doors.

When I became eligible to use this sanctum years later, I never went near it, unless I wanted to throw up. If I can't pee with the people I won't pee at all!

In 1936 Bates went to Benton and Bowles, with Wonder Bread on a leash; Roy Durstine called him "disloyal." I did not know what he meant, nor do I now. Why should Theodore L. Bates be loyal to Roy S. Durstine, or for that matter to BBDO? The only thing that made me sore was that Ted did not ask me to come along.

I did send him the man he wanted a few years later. Rosser Reeves was leaving Ruthrauff and Ryan, an agency famous for successful direct mail advertising. I invited him over, and hired him for $6,000, probably more than I was getting. He accepted, but came back again next week. Bates had offered him $15,000. But he had promised to come with me, and would, if I insisted.

"Say Hello to Ted," I said. "And run along. I don't want anybody around here looking at me with sad eyes and thinking,

'There's the man who wouldn't let me make fifteen thousand dollars.' And by the way, ask Ted if he has any more of those fifteen-thousand-dollar jobs."

Together Rosser and Ted originated the "Knock 'em down and drag 'em out" school of advertising that brought millions fast, Fast, FAST relief from almost anything. It worked fine for thirty years.

Chet Bowles was a writer on Wonder Bread, as was I, although neither of us worked for the other. His headlines always began with "Madam." "Madam, please try . . ." "Madam, we guarantee." It did not bother Chet a bit that there are various kinds of Madams. Maybe he had made a survey and found that certain Madams eat more bread than law-abiding ladies.

As I came into Batten, J. Stirling Getchell walked out, leaving notes on everybody's desk: "I've had enough!" It is probably apocryphal that he kept demanding more and more up to $50,-000 a year to keep the Colgate account in Batten. All I know is that it left when he left, although, strangely enough, it never went with him, nor did it ever go to him later.

"Getch" eventually started the hottest hot shop that ever existed. He did the earliest Plymouth and De Soto advertising as well as Mobil Oil, which was then known as Socony-Vacuum. He also achieved what no other agency, to my knowledge, has ever done. Clients of competitive agencies forced their agencies to pay Getchell a fee for his opinion of their current advertising. Like some other great admen, he was a little thin on research. When asked how he knew a campaign would work, he answered, "Because I feel it in my guts!" Of course there were a lot more guts around then than now.

Much later, he tried to hire me, at least I think that is what he was trying to do. First, drinks and dinner at his Waldorf suite. Then talk until 1 A.M. Suddenly he said, "I'd like you to see the campaign the boys are working on." At 1 A.M.? He phoned his shop, and, sure enough, a dozen gnomes trotted over with layouts, proofs, radio tapes, the works.

How did I like them?

I liked them fine, but I had no yen to be in his shop working at 1 A.M. and have everything taken away just to show some guy Getch was having dinner with. He died at a little over forty.

Some said he knew he had a bad heart and was racing against time to lay away enough money for his family.

When the going got real tough somebody fired Charlie Mortimer, later president and chairman of General Foods. It seems as though there were a policy of throwing out the talented guys and hanging onto the bums. I am not unconscious of what that says about me, but I was saved because a penny came up heads instead of tails.

When Bill Benton first joined the Batten Company, he found that Monday always started with a meeting at which various big men in the agency spoke.

Bill, who believed that opportunity strikes sooner and harder if you goose it along a bit, found out who was in charge of these meetings.

"Someday," Bill told the meetings man, "a speaker may not be able to show up. Put me down as a standby. I have a speech all ready."

Bill got his chance in a few months. He told them that the Batten Company was years behind in its thinking, that they were too satisfied with mediocrity, and no match at all with a modern agency like Lord and Thomas (now Foote, Cone, and Belding), an agency that seemed to be getting all the accounts that came loose, and did what Bill considered brilliant work.

Bill wrote his mother that some people got up and left in the middle of his talk. Others stayed but openly disagreed. He probably had plenty of sympathizers who were afraid to open their mouths. But in his own words, "Everybody knows who Billy Benton is."

Bill might have been a little less excited about Lord and Thomas had he heard Albert Lasker, head of that agency, tell Mr. Johns the secret of his and his company's success.

"Watch the ads, and listen to the radio," he advised. "When you hear or see advertising that you consider great, find out who is responsible for it. Offer him twice his salary. Work him hard, squeeze him like a lemon. When he runs dry, fire him, and get someone else."

This did not seem like cricket to Mr. Johns's Episcopalian choir-leading mind. I am sure that the idea of doubling anyone's salary was equally repulsive. I can personally guarantee that only once did the Batten Company double anyone's salary.

After Benton's speech, lightning from the front office did not strike him dead—but some thought they heard distant thunder. If Bill was fired for suggesting a merger with BDO, it must have been because he was treading on ground already sacred to Mr. Johns.

The three partners of the agency three floors below us were not yet a dozen years out of college. In the nine years of their existence as an agency they had compiled a list of over ninety clients. They did, indeed, get new business faster than they could handle it.

If they had trouble at BDO, and they did, it was Roy Durstine's lack of organizing ability. He believed in the "all-round adman." The idea that all advertising men should be equally gifted in all jobs to be done, is silly on the surface. Yet BDO had no copy department—and after the merger BBDO had none.

Tragically, Roy Durstine believed he was an "all-round adman" and if he could be, so could anyone else. He was wrong twice.

The unfriendly skies of 1930.

Flying over a haystack on a hot day is worse than hitting an unexpected hole in the road with a car, according to Fred Nichols who flew from Columbus to Kansas City, T.A.T. one of those days when it was 107 on the ground below. A column of moist heated air rises from the haystack and, if one of the wings passes over it, the plane is tilted sideways and comes down with a terrific edgewise jolt into the cooler air on the other side. As haystacks are about the most plentiful objects to be found in Kansas, the pilot is kept busy turning out for them. Fred says the trip was interesting, but by no means the most comfortable way to go.

Nature abhors a vacuum, and an empty window office.

# That Wonderful Year— 1891

## 7

☞ People always ask, "Did God create BBDO alone, or did Bruce Barton help him?" I intend to clear up this question once and for all.

You remember 1891! That was the year the Kaiser paid a state visit to London. There were frantic demonstrations of Franco-Russian Friendship. The Czar listened to the *Marseillaise*, played from the deck of a French battleship at Kronstadt. And George Batten, Ad Manager of Funk and Wagnalls, decided to do a bit of moonlighting and opened what must have been the world's smallest agency. Thirty seems to have been his magic number. His address was 30 Park Row, his office was thirty (some say thirty-eight) feet wide, and he paid thirty dollars a month rent. His staff was Marjorie F. Hopkins, then still in pigtails, who stayed with him until he died. Each evening, and often it was quite late, Batten would escort her to the safety of the subway, then walk to the Jersey tubes. Batten was nearing sixty but those who knew him best said, "He lived on swamproot," and, "His new business shoes haven't worn out yet."

He snared the MacBeth Chimney account. Not exactly a growth account, chimneys for kerosene lamps—but it still exists as a part of Corning Glass.

Next came Zenith Horse Collars—"More power for every horse" —and where were you, Federal Trade Commission, when we needed you most? To show that he was not partial to horses, he was appointed by Sterilac Sanitary Milk Pails. I do not know the nature of these pails but I assume from my farm experience that there was some device that prevented the cow from putting her foot into it, a typical bovine gesture.

In about a year William H. Johns joined him. Fifty years later there would be a great banquet held for Mr. Johns where the theme (and yelling) conveyed the message that "Fifty Years of Johns is not Enough." He agreed and lived three more years.

Batten had a couple of formulas for good advertising. The first was:

> Describe the product
> Tell what it will do
> Ask people to buy it

And the second:

> A good advertisement must be good enough to attract attention, yet so neat in appearance that it will not offend good taste. The language should be plain and brief and it should be published in the paper read by the people most likely to buy the product advertised.

For the tiny staff he quoted Shakespeare:

> Our doubts are traitors and make us lose the good we oft might win by fearing the attempt.

Despite his handicap of self-imposed honesty, despite a very thin income the first year ($2,500), and despite the panic at the turn of the century, he was crowing mightily by 1905: "From one employee in 1891 to nearly 50 now, from an annual expense account of $1500 to $75,000 indicates *growth*. And we've just begun!"

In 1897 he began issuing *The Wedge*, a tiny magazine that went to clients and prospects. He actually sold space in it! He was generous with his editorial advice to everyone, from his competitors to President McKinley. He favored calm in the face of the approaching war with Spain:

> Everyone seems to think that the moment war is declared, business will stop and the Spanish will occupy our East Coast cities. Even Egg Harbor has petitioned to have its Harbor mined. Today war, as an element of business, is entirely removed except to make it better.

Batten was helpful to prospects as well:

> Royal Baking Powder suggests a can of Royal as a wedding present. If such a caper were ever to become a custom we are afraid it would raise more Hades than biscuits.

And how is this for attending to someone else's business:

> For a multiform illustration of what an advertisement should not be, and for a fine example of how a splendid business can make headway in spite of its advertising, we commend you to Huyler's.

Being a good churchman who preferred to employ people from families of "the pulpit or the plow," he had nothing but holy wrath for those advertisers who parodied sacred text, such as the manufacturer of floor finish who parodied the litany:

> *From the slippery wax floor*
>   *Stainflor delivers us*
> *From the scratched varnished floor*
>   *Stainflor delivers us*
> *From the cracked shellacked floor*
>   *Stainflor delivers us. . . .*

Most agencies, even though they may do wonderful work for their clients, do a poor job of advertising themselves. An agency loses all objectivity when it becomes its own client. George Batten was no exception. Did he follow his own formula for advertising when he advertised the George Batten Company? Not a bit of it!

His advertising theme for his own company was "We Go Anywhere for Business." Jeering competitors drove him into explanation:

We go anywhere in reason to places of respectability on any mission that is honorable. We could not go to San Francisco for a half-page. We do not go into saloons or other questionable rendezvous. And we do not go to the golf links, or the theater, or the opera, or any other place of amusement to inveigle business under the guise of false friendship.

From old pictures, Batten looked like Teddy Roosevelt seen through the wrong end of a telescope. Same mustache. Same glasses balanced on his nose. He, too, carried a big stick, and ruled on everything, including female dress—no "peek-a-boo" waists, no "rats" to prop up the hair. One girl saved up for weeks to buy a set of rats and got them too late to wear to the office.

Batten believed that a clear desk meant a clear mind, and he stayed in at noontime making clear minds by sweeping everything off of desks onto the floor. One brave soul is quoted as saying: "Pick it up yourself or hire someone else to do it!" But jobs were scarce and few rebelled.

He even sent around a notice, "No more smoking in the office." Just before the revolution broke, Mr. Johns strolled out of his office with a large cigar in his mouth and asked loudly, "Has anybody got a match?" The subject was never mentioned again.

The temperament of this ancient agency shows through the memos that one Mr. Reeves, the office manager, sent around constantly:

This office will be closed on Friday (Columbus Day) but will be open on Saturday as usual.

Your attention is called to the fact that the lunch period is from 12:30 to 1:30. This rule is not being observed strictly enough.

If you are late, make out a late slip immediately, giving a valid reason, not an excuse, and hand it to your department head immediately.

Once more I remind you to use pins instead of paper clips. Papers do not get lost when pinned together.

Batten could not remember names. So he called every male "Harry," except Frank the Boy. Batten lurked in his office like a spider, and occasionally scuttled out, seizing some luckless wight by the lapels and asking, "In what year was Lincoln born?" Even if the man knew the answer, he was stricken with paralysis.

Batten would throw a small tantrum.

"Fools!" he would cry as he strode through the office, "All fools! Who is to perpetuate this business when I am gone?" The answer was striding right behind him, his big face glowing and his big cigar likewise.

Batten ordered that the first hour of each day be devoted to answering mail and cleaning up details. Another hour each day, not specified, was to be spent reading the World's Masters of Literature, which Batten provided, for, "How can you give it out if you haven't taken it in?"

Some people thought little of this idea of stimulating a taste for literature in advertising copywriters. One was Christopher Morley, who wrote a "literary ad" for the subway:

## CALIBAN IN THE SUBWAY

WILL BUFFET: (*while guard plaineth grievously, "Allow them egress, passage to emerge"*)

*Pragmatic chap, that guard, a Harvard man?*
*Buffet, I say, an illicit entry*
*Flatteneth elbows closely to his flanks*
*And foldeth paper longwise (in a way*
*Subwastral hath devised)*
*Fasteneth one eye on Mutt and Jeff*
*The other eye? Lawks! Keep it alit*
*For the advertising cards or maybe female beauty*
*The knowing rouge; and thus while Urbs, the town,*
*Bitterly debronxeth every morn*
*He, wedged, compressed, pulped almost in a throng*
*Buffeteth ribs and hams and shanks and shins*
*Of other sturdy cits impinged upon him—*

*Impinged? Maybe the word is not strong enough*
*Feeleth upon his spine some knobbly elbow*
*Also, about his ear, a pompion plant*
*Or egret worn on some caste lady's hat*
*Creeps in to tickle; he regretteth the egret—*
*Ha. More than that, a noisesome waft of garlic*
*From some sallow dark complexion (whose, he wonders)*
*So intimately quoined against his cheek*
*Deploreth four out of five have pyorrhea*
*Dense in the hodge-podge, fixed, surmiseth germs*
*Aye. Flu, perhaps. Grabbeth an atomizer*
*Times Square. Hollah. Prithee grant me exit*
*Gramercy, friend—and maketh escapement sweet*
*Turnstile clappeth him gently astern*
*Gingerly feeleth his debruised corpus*
*No broken bones (Huzza) thanketh the Lord*
*Who made him tough and burley and not too plastic*
*But thinketh dolefully, God help the women.*

Among the many things Batten hated were Germans. He declared war somewhat ahead of the United States. When the *Lusitania* was torpedoed and sunk he called a meeting of the organization, and fired every unmarried man of military age.

"Your country needs you more than I do."

Overcome by his own patriotism he banged his turnip watch on the desk until it gave up and flipped its guts over the entire front row.

Batten died on Saturday, February 16, 1918, probably from too much acid in his battery.

Somewhere there is an oil painting of him by Ike Hazelton. Batten rejected it indignantly. Finally Hazelton figured out what was wrong. He painted in the ribbon he had forgotten, the lapel ribbon that showed Mr. George Batten to be a Son of the American Revolution. That made the picture perfect!

For years this picture hung in various offices around the agency. The rumor was that the lads who drank their lunch at the Ritz-Carlton bar across the street, played a word game known as "Ghost." The loser got Mr. Batten's picture until next they met.

Finally, it disappeared altogether. It was said that some man who retired took it with him. We have put no detectives on his trail and made no effort to recapture the picture.

George Batten was all right for his time, if a bit eccentric. But there was no radio then, no TV, no Bill Bernbach, no David Ogilvy. No Mary Wells. No Federal Trade Commission. But it seems unlikely that he would have survived the complexities and competition of today.

*The following comes to you live from Frank the Boy, who was there . . .*

When I joined Batten in 1910 I was fifteen and the company had just moved to 381 Fourth. We were right across from the old Madison Square Garden, the one designed by Stanford White, the fellow who got shot by Harry Thaw on account of Evelyn Nesbitt, and there were always naked men sunning themselves on the roof. You could hit them with a paper clip if you had a strong rubber band and figured the wind drift just right.

We had an art department of four people. Two of them could draw and two of them could think. There were nine or ten copywriters, including one poor fellow who always walked backward. He couldn't stand getting anybody behind him, but of course everybody tried to, and he broke a couple of windows by backing into them. But he never fell through.

In the art department there was a little tank with a couple of those twenty-five-cent turtles. One of the artists, Beverly Bodley, painted "Lehn" on the back of one and "Fink" on the back of the other, and these turtles were supposed to glare at Starling Busser, the account executive on Lehn and Fink, whenever he went by and worry him because the president of Lehn and Fink might come in and see them and take the account away.

We errand boys had a wonderful thing. You know a magazine has to have a written insertion order before it can run an ad. Well, these orders were so precious we wouldn't think of sending them through the mails. And anyway, all the magazines, or their representatives, were in New York, and we errand boys delivered them personally. We got a nickel for each call we made, and we picked up quite a few nickels. Using transfers, we could go by trolley across twenty-third to Eighth Avenue, to Spring and MacDougal Streets, where Butterick was, down to Fourteenth Street, down Broadway, across and down Sixth all for one nickel. 150 Nassau Street and 38 Park Row is the same building, but we used to give both addresses and get two nickels. Everything was fine until I got promoted to the mail department.

I was a pretty fresh kid then. You know how Mr. Batten called all the boys "Harry" because he liked Harry Holloway and couldn't remember names? So once he yelled "Harry" at me and I kept right on going. He ran after me, grabbed me by the shoulder and spun me around and asked if I had heard him. I told him I had heard him call Harry but my name wasn't Harry, it was Frank. He said, "As far as I am concerned, your name is 'Harry,' and when I call 'Harry,' that means you!" So I was Harry.

We had our own print shop, God knows why. The printers were all union men, except the head printer, and Mr. Batten couldn't do a thing with them. The head printer didn't have to be a union man, because he could lick anyone in the shop, and Mr. Wyckoff, our very religious treasurer, always gave him Mondays off to get over Sunday. Well, we'd send any new kid in to this monkey for "a handful of half tone dots" and he'd say to the kid, "Hold out yer goddam hand." Then he'd slap a big gob of gooky ink all over the kid's hand and the whole office would laugh because it was very funny. The printers always had some half-wit kid as a printer's devil, and they'd send him to the saloon next door every morning with tin cans hung on a long pole. For beer, you know. And when they'd get a new kid they'd send him in to see if Mr. Batten wanted "Light" or "Dark." Mr. Batten would knock the cans all over the place, growl and shout, "If this is the nonsensical way this place is being run, I'll put a stop to it at once!" He'd scare the kid senseless, but he couldn't do anything about the printers because of the union.

Did I tell you the time we were *loaned* an account? It was the W. K. Kellogg Company of Battle Creek, and they had at that time, as I remember, a "house agency," which meant they would call their own advertising department an agency, and keep all the commissions.

Mr. Kellogg wanted to go to Europe for a while, and Mr. Batten and Mr. Johns had such a reputation for honesty that he asked them to take care of his advertising while he was away, just like you might ask someone to take care of your dog while you were away. Well, it was a big account, at least half a million, unheard of in those days. Mr. Johns' desk, of course, was heaped with flowers and signs all over, too. "Congratulations!" "Wonderful work!"—that sort of thing.

It was decided to hold a great contest for Kellogg, to get the best artists in America to draw pictures of healthy kids. The prize was $1,500 because Mr. Batten did not want any ordinary cheap contest. So many pictures came in that he had to hire storage space down on the sixth floor, and a very nice young chap in our bookkeeping department who belonged to the "Hudson Dusters" told Mr. Wyckoff that he would get a man to guard all this art. This lug just locked himself in all day with the artwork and a can or two of beer. There was a secret knock and you could join. It was quite a club until Mr. Wyckoff discovered it. Robley Feland was sort of second man in the copy department. We never had what you'd call a copy chief, but Hal Briney was the head man. One day Batten told Briney that he needed him in our Chicago office. Briney said, "Why should I go to Chicago?" and Batten said, "Because you can either go there or draw your pay!" So Briney went, and Robley Feland became head of copy, or whatever you might call it.

He was considered to be a very good writer but he used to drive people nuts by saying, "I won't be in this afternoon. I am going to sit in the park," and you'd say, "What park?" and he'd say, "Belmont, of course." And this would drive you frantic because you were already late with a campaign. "Don't worry," he'd say, "it's all done." And when you asked him where the hell it was then, he'd point to his pink hair and say, "Right up there!" A queer guy all right!

Pretty soon after I came to Batten I started "Going Through the Woods." This meant that I was going to the Wood Secretarial School, because I wanted to better myself.

I could make big glorious flourishes but nobody on God's green earth could read them.

So one day I hear that Mr. Batten, Mr. Johns, and Mr. Little are going to Buffalo after a piece of new business and they wanted me to go along. I said why didn't they carry their own damn packages but not so loud that someone might hear me. A new business presentation then was a lot of pictures—"This is our Art Department."

But—my gosh—when we got ready to leave, another kid was carrying the packages. It didn't figure at all.

What I discovered next morning was shocking—they had heard that I was going to secretarial school, and they wanted me to take down all their speeches so they could be printed in the Newsletter for everybody to admire. Naturally I did the best I could but nobody could take down Mr. Batten. He just har-r--r-umphed and mumbled and I was so scared anyway that my hand shook all over the place.

When I got back to the office a few days later, I stared at my notes a full hour and the tears started rolling down my cheeks. So Miss Hopkins, Batten's secretary who was always trying to mother me, came running over, because a big boy like me crying meant only one thing—a death in the family. She was disgusted with me when she found out what was the matter and said, "Give me those notes," and she looked at them and said, "Oh, my God," although Miss Hopkins would never actually say it that way.

I started to put my little bunch of things together and I was going to quit because there was nothing else to do as anyone could see. But Miss Hopkins called Miss Powell, who was Mr. Johns's secretary and Miss Hatch, who was Mr. Little's secretary. They put their heads together and said, "All right, Boy, we'll save your hide this one more time." And each one wrote her boss's speech that night, just guessing from knowing their bosses and what they would have said. And they must have done pretty good, too, because all three of the speeches were printed and there hasn't been a complaint in almost sixty years.

How about that, huh?

The old George Batten Company had a convention of clients on November 11 and 12, 1919. According to the menu, dessert was a "bombe" but apparently everything else was okay.

George Batten ad in *Scribner's*, July 1893:
I am after success—my clients', which is my own.
George Batten instruction:
Set it in simple plain type . . . it will stand out like a Quaker on Broadway.

One of the most delicate chores around the shop in the old days was explaining to innocent lady copywriters why their headlines could not be used. One, I remember, was for Hostess Cake: "Now Dorothy has a party *every* night!" Another, introducing colored toilet paper: "The final touch of Loveliness."

# Papa
# Johns

*8*

☞ When William H. Johns (the man nobody ever called "Bill"), three years out of CCNY and twenty-two years out of Cornwall, England, joined the George Batten Company in 1892, the first thing he did was write a letter to his mother.

". . . Saturday morning I had a talk with Mr. Batten in which he reiterated his desire to have me, and offered me $10 a week to start and the regular commission of 15% on all the money I bring in. This is really more than I should have dared to ask for. It looks as though your little boy had met his chance and soon will be able to pay back his dear parents for all the kindnesses they have showered upon him . . ."

Sort of reminds you of the letters kids write their dear parents today, doesn't it?

His next letter contained a careful inventory of his strengths, his weaknesses and what he intended to do about them. His self-portrait would have fit him as well at seventy-three as it did at twenty-three.

"I am in the advertising business," he wrote. "All around me are men more brilliant than I am, other men with wider acquaintance than I, and still others with more experience than I. With what am I endowed whereby I can cope in this highly competitive field? One thing I have that not all others have. I happen to be gifted with an unusual physique. I am never ill and seldom weary. I can and will work longer hours. What I lack in brilliance I can make up in study and knowledge of our business. If I lack acquaintance, I will put in more time getting to know people. What I lack in experience I will acquire by working harder—and I will become more experienced in more hours and fewer years than my competitors."

It was an accurate description of a bulldozer. Only once in recorded history was he ever late. That was three years before he joined Batten. He explained that even the horse cars were not running. That was March 12, 1888, still remembered on that day each year by a thinning cult of "Blizzard Men."

Shortly he was out of Batten again. His first job was to produce a booklet for Funk and Wagnalls, advertising their paper *The Voice*. Johns did not consider himself a better writer than Robert Burns, so he took for his title "Oh, wad some power the giftie gie us to see oursels as others see us." Johns made nine mistakes in one title and ninety-and-nine hundred Scots we hae their Bobby read, rose and wrote in righteous wrath. Nobody blamed him for stealing, but only for stealing inexactly.

Blair and Company, bankers, employed Johns for a couple of years. But Batten missed him, invited him to lunch with him at the old Astor House, near where the Woolworth Building now stands, and signed him to a new contract which differed from the original in two places. Johns was guaranteed a minimum of $1,000 a year. And he was offered an opportunity to buy an interest in the company later, "should his services prove satisfactory."

Advertising was a mess at that time; advertising practices, George Batten reported, "were as crooked as a ram's horn." Even the combined virtue of Batten and Johns, a fearsome total, was not enough to keep the rest of the world honest. To top it all off, the business world went into a bathyspherical economic dive, compared with which the "big" depression of the thirties was like a dip in the clubhouse pool. Profits for August 1903 were $17.94. But the two plugged on with the faith that comes from having no other choice.

Johns was above all a "solicitor." Since his yearly income could best be fattened by getting new business, Johns went after it like a retriever after a downed duck.

One cornered prospect in Boston begged him, "Mr. Johns, will you please take your magnetic personality out of here and go back to New York so I can *think?*"

Every time Johns got a new account he would find his desk covered with flowers next morning. Everyone stood up and cheered.

Sometimes, even then, unsolicited business "came in over the transom." In 1909 a letter came from the Webster Company:

*Gentlemen:*
*We would like you to prepare some printed advertising to run in a Philadelphia publication. I believe its name is the Saturday Evening Post. Temporarily you are our agency. We will see what develops.*

Fifty years later a small banquet was held to celebrate the fact that our temporary client was still with us.

One prospect in Duluth said he did not need an advertising agency. What he needed was someone to replace his ailing church organist on Sunday.

"Besides," he grumped, "I wrote George Batten and he never answered."

"I am the answer," said Johns.

"I suppose you play the organ, too!"

That was easy for Johns, who not only played the organ but led the choir at All Saints Church in Bayside, L.I. He played the organ on Sunday and "got the order" on Monday.

George Batten got so excited about this achievement that he wired Johns he was changing the name of the company from George Batten Company to George Batten *and* Company. This mighty alteration never took place. I find no evidence of it after going through a considerable amount of browning and cracking Batten material.

The president of the Ostermoor Mattress Company ("Built, not stuffed"), got Johns on the phone. He had committed himself to one half-page in *Munsey's Magazine* and now repented of it.

"Johns, I told you I would spend that money for advertising but you know as well as I do that I might as well throw it down the sewer. Why don't you and I take our wives to Atlantic City, blow the money in that way. Then we'll at least have something to show for it."

"Nothing doing," said Johns at somewhat greater length.

"I'll bet you a Dunlap hat that I never hear anything from this advertising but your bill."

Within three weeks Johns had the hat. Ostermoor had already received four orders. The fact that the advertisement had not yet run adds a piquant note of mystery.

Johns, of course, had regular clients to serve. One of them, Sol N. Rosenbloom ("A prince of a man"), said to Johns, "You are walking up here (to the National Cloak and Suit Company) and back to the Potter Building every day. They say these telephones work pretty well. If you'll put one in, I will, and we'll see how they work." They must have worked, we still have them.

Among Johns's prospects was a man named Fred Johnson, whose office was at 99 Chambers Street. He made Iver Johnson bicycles and revolvers, and was altogether a rather abrasive character. His current advertising showed two babies in a crib, playing with a presumably loaded Iver Johnson revolver. The copy explained that the revolver could not be accidentally discharged. Johnson asked Johns what he thought of it. There must have been many good evasive answers, but Johns did not know what evasion meant.

"I think it's all a lie! No revolver is that safe!"

Johnson grabbed a revolver from his desk drawer, jumped up and yelled, "Follow me." Johns must have been the first and only man ever to follow a man who was obviously angry, and carried a loaded revolver, into a basement. Obediently he hung his coat over an empty packing case.

Johnson threw the revolver against an old rusty safe. He threw it against the ceiling and banged it on the floor. He slammed it against the wall. He sat down, aimed the revolver at his own knee and pounded the hammer with a carpenter's hammer.

"Now are you satisfied?"

"Yes," Johns admitted, "if it's loaded!"

Johnson released the safety catch and fired five shots through a packing case and also through Johns's coat, hanging on the other side. Even Johns could see the new theme, "Hammer the Hammer."

He came back to the office highly elated, and well ventilated. His diplomacy had "got the order."

When I first knew Johns he had attained full maturity at 250 pounds. He was a big man and he liked big things. Big pencils, big pens, a big desk in a big office. And when he ate alone in the old Roosevelt Grill, as he often did, he always ordered a big cup of coffee and a big slice of pie in spite of the fact that these things are as standardized as though they were stamped out by machinery.

Johns was not the type of man who knows the face but can't recall the name. He remembered neither. Faced with this memory problem he would fight for time by repeating, "Well! Well! Well!" until someone took him off the hook.

Once when he saw a man sneaking in late, he shouted at the young man with an oversized brief case: "Draw your pay and get out!" Nobody ever told him that he had fired the office bootlegger, and that young man was too frightened to show up in the office ever again. We had to go to *him*.

It never occurred to Mr. Johns that he was not an American. Being born in Cornwall, England, tended to make him an Englishman. He merrily voted for every President since Cleveland. It was only when he applied for a passport that the Feds caught up with him.

There was considerable "Kaff-kaffing, harruphing" and other forms of laryngeal oratory, before he consented to fill out the necessary forms and have Oscar, his chauffeur, drive him downtown. He was instantly in trouble.

Asked, "Do you forswear allegiance to George the Fifth, King of England?" Johns replied:

"I certainly do not."

"But why not?"

"I never had any allegiance, so how can I forswear something I never had?"

"This makes things very difficult!"

"Yes, it does," Mr. Johns agreed.

Nevertheless, he came back a citizen, carrying his little American flag.

In a talk over WOR on the contributions of advertising to our civilization he said, "The ladies will all agree that a nation composed largely of bewhiskered males has become clean-shaven and better looking as a result of advertising the improvements in razors and the reduced cost of razors and blades." (Please, Mr. Johns, don't come back right now.)

On the tenth anniversary of my servitude, I was called into his office to receive the traditional Hamilton watch.

"Your tenth anniversary, I believe."

"Yes, sir."

He handed me the watch.

"But it is also an important fifth anniversary, Mr. Johns."

"Fifth? I do not understand."

"It's the fifth anniversary of the day you stopped calling me 'Doug Manson.'"

People of Mr. Johns's era wasted little time debating whether they had to use client products or not. They had to. Albert Lasker was strolling the aisles of Lord and Thomas when he spotted a pack of Philip Morris on a luckless wight's desk. They should have been Lucky Strike, of course.

"Just what is that?" Lasker regarded the pack as though it were a fish too long dead. The terrified underling had what he thought was an excuse.

"I smoke Luckies, sir. I must have picked these up by mistake. My wife smokes Philip Morris."

"And your wife, I presume, has an independent income?"

It was Mr. Johns who held the all-time client-loyalty record.

We got a small bit of Goodyear truck tire advertising. Mr. Johns's Pierce-Arrows immediately shed their tires and appeared with Goodyears all around. Somehow the Goodyear account came unstuck and we were appointed by Firestone. Off with the Goodyears, on with the Firestones.

But the ageing Harvey Firestone turned out to be an advertising genius and the trains to and from Florida were filled with BBDOers—half going south to learn just what he wanted, the other half going north trying to figure out what they had heard. Only Mr. Firestone could write phrases like "For One Week Only." Only Mr. Firestone could find type black enough. Shortly before we all became nervous wrecks, we resigned the account. It was an honest resignation, not the more usual kind made two jumps ahead of the ax. It was a brave cutting of our own throat. Four million dollars! It still hurts on rainy days.

Along came B. F. Goodrich, due in part to Alex Osborn's friendship for John Collyer, president of Goodrich. Will anyone who can't guess what tires next went on Mr. Johns's Pierce-Arrows please stand up.

We had, at that time, an account named Hampton House. They decorated or redecorated the homes of people who could afford them. Mr. Johns sent his wife to Europe. As a nice surprise for her he had the house completely done over from cellar to attic. This pleased Mrs. Johns so much that she collapsed and was never quite the same the rest of her life.

Johns also memoed the organization turgidly and frequently on the subject of using our clients' products. Read one:

> In making your personal purchases does it ever occur to you that you owe your firm a responsibility in doing your part to promote the prosperity of our clients? Every man should shave with a Gillette, and when we buy ginger ale refuse any brand but Cliquot Club. We should wear Arrow collars and specify Ethyl in our Socony. This memo was prompted by the news that one of our men recently bought a Ford.

Such memos are futile. I sent out none when I was president. I merely let word be circulated that, in my opinion, a man who did not use client products when he could was a damned fool. And the history of damned fools in our company was not an attractive one.

As commodore of the Bayside Yacht Club, Mr. Johns wore all the regalia including the gold spaghetti on the visor of his cap. He rated three toots from ocean liners. And he took his responsibilities seriously. One of these was to fire the sunset gun, unless someone anchored in the same port outranked him—an unlikely possibility. Commodore Johns often anchored at Lloyd Harbor, a place where people go who do not like to drink on land. Johns did not like to drink at all and flew no cocktail flag. His guests were always making trips between the deck and their cabins.

You do not fire the sunset gun at approximately sunset—you

fire it at the split second of official sunset. Mr. Johns had the crew bring the little cannon up on deck, assemble it, load it and hand him the lanyard. He was watching his chronometer closely . . . just five seconds more, but . . . bal-oo-oo-oo-m! Some liquorified fellow paying attention to neither time nor protocol had fired the sunset gun.

Mr. Johns swore his most frightful oath, "Fiddlesticks." The little cannon was taken below to await a better day.

It is hard to tell, at this far time, which stories of Mr. Johns are true and which are apocryphal. I always hoped that this one was true. He had watched the kids around his neighborhood folding little dartlike paper planes and sailing them over the lawn. One day when his door was closed and he was not busy, he folded one and it looker authentic enough. Windows were open in those pre-air-conditioned days, so he sailed it out of the window, and stuck his head out just enough to see what happened. It dropped ten stories straight down, leveled off at about six feet, and zipped right into the face of the traffic cop who presided over Madison and Forty-sixth. Mr. Johns retracted his head like a terrified turtle, uttered a few "Oh, dear's," and decided to get to work.

Not too long afterward the policeman walked into Mr. Johns's office carrying the wrecked plane in his hand.

"Aren't you a bit old for this sort of thing?"

Mr. Johns had made the plane out of his own stationery, which included name, address and title.

One day Mr. Johns had to find a substitute organist for All Saints Church. He couldn't play because he had to lend his daughter Betty a fatherly arm as she marched up the aisle.

As he did, one sentimental lady was heard to say: "We're thinking of changing the name of All Saints, you know. It really should be St. Johns."

Mr. Johns, one of the world's most persistent Gilbert and Sullivan fans, wrote a musical comedy himself once. It was named *Micrimania,* and was performed at All Saints Church, Bayside, L.I. Among those who attended were A. W. Erickson, whose agency later merged with M. K. McCann Co. to form McCann-Erickson. Mr. Erickson brought as his guest the great Victor Herbert. After the show Victor Herbert was rumored to have said, "It was a great day for the stage when Mr. Johns went into advertising." But then it was Mr. Erickson who quoted him thus, and he was a competitor.

---

November 18, 1920:

E. T. Meredith, Secretary of Agriculture, says, "The man who fails to advertise just because conditions are a little uncertain is on a par with the farmer who refuses to feed his cows because the price of butter has gone down."

# Oysters
# for three

# 9

☞ Three men, left jobless by the armistice that ended World War I, met at the Grand Central Oyster Bar to talk things over. Two of the men, Roy Durstine and Alex Osborn, had been agency men before the war, and thought only of getting back into it. The third, Bruce Barton, had no agency experience and little desire to get any. The only thing he was sure of—he was never going back into magazine editing. He would rather starve.

Bruce Barton, although he probably knew nothing of it, had almost been considered by George Batten as a writer. J. P. Knapp was the publisher of *Every Week*, a magazine that was going down for the third time because of paper costs, and high labor costs caused by World War I. Many years later he started *This Week*, which also sank from sight.

In 1915 he was calling on Mr. Johns to get some business for his quaking publication.

"I think you ought to hire my editor, Bruce Barton," Mr. Knapp said. "He isn't thirty yet, but he is smart and a good writer!"

As soon as Knapp left, Johns hurried into Batten's office with the glad tidings.

"What can he do?" asked Batten.

"He is reputed to be able to write."

"How much will he cost us?"

"Ten thousand dollars."

"Why, Mr. Johns," said Batten, who in twenty-five years had never called him Bill, "that's a lot more than you make!"

"I know," said Johns. "But I figure that, if we get Barton, I'll make more money, too!"

"Forget it," Batten answered, "I never spent ten thousand dollars for a writer, and I never will!"

Now, at the oyster bar, Durstine was telling Bruce that advertising was a pleasant way for a writer to earn more than he deserved. But Alex, who had worked for the Remington Agency in Buffalo, had his own problem—he wanted to live in Buffalo. People do, you know! Alex Osborn therefore took himself out of the picture. It was agreed that the other two would set up Barton and Durstine. Bruce was to work for half days only, leaving him time for other writing. He wanted nothing to do with hiring, or firing, or any part of managing either. Salaries were set at $5,000, which Osborn thought a bit high.

Listen, if you will, to Harford Powel, a man who was there:

I went there to ask Bruce Barton to write for *Collier's*. He was sitting there, looking overworked and anxious, in a small cluttered set of rooms on the top floor of 25 West 45th Street. His partner, Durstine, was ill with pneumonia. There were some chaps about, but the only one with previous advertising experience was Frank Hubbard. He was making the contracts, keeping the books, interviewing the applicants, bossing the help and wrapping up electros in his spare time after dinner. Put it down to Hubbard's good housekeeping, to Barton's amazing ability to meet, interest and satisfy important people, and most of all to Durstine's skill as an organizer that, in four years from this modest beginning BDO has been appointed by 98 advertisers including such glittering examples as General Motors, General Electric, National Biscuit Company and American Radiator.

By Powel's reference to BDO you can tell that "B&D" had been unable to get along without "O." Osborn was taken into partnership. He could stay in Buffalo and run the Buffalo office.

Another interesting comment was made when BDO moved out of 25 West Forty-fifth. The elevator man said, "I don't know who can replace them unless Barnum and Bailey moves their winter quarters down here from Bridgeport!"

Bruce, who hated management and swore he would have no part of it, was made president. Roy Durstine was vice-president and general manager. Alex was vice-president in charge of Buffalo.

It sounds like a setup designed by Rube Goldberg, but it had plenty of what was then called "Moxie." None were out of their thirties. Yet Bruce, through his magazine work, knew everyone that counted in business and politics. Osborn proved his worth even in Buffalo by bringing in the General Baking account. Durstine, the "all-round adman"—didn't mind working all night or several nights in a row when necessary. In four years, as Powel says, BDO had built a list of ninety-eight accounts. They not only won accounts, but created them where none had existed before.

There was a group of electrical equipment manufacturers, loosely joined by the legal name General Electric. But they did not use the GE name on products. Their electric lamps, for instance, were named Edison Mazda. Bruce wanted everything they made to be named General Electric, so that customer satisfaction with one kind of product would build confidence in another.

"It's a damned shame," Bruce said, "that the only place you can see GE is on the motorman's box of a trolley car!" He did a campaign to show them what he meant. He called GE "The Initials of a Friend."

For General Motors he prepared a booklet entitled "The Lees of Virginia." It was *something* to be named Lee. But it was a lot more to be one of the "Lees of Virginia." Making the name General Motors have the same acceptance would benefit every car. The head of Cadillac figured that his car had all the standing it needed and would only suffer by being publicly a brother of

Chevrolet. But when the campaign was accepted and running, it seemed to benefit Chevrolet without hurting Cadillac in the least.

Why did not these companies see the answer themselves? Why did they need an advertising man to tell them? The answer is the real reason for having agencies—the manufacturer sees his job as pushing the product at the consumer, the agency sees things from the consumer's viewpoint. It wants to create consumer pull, instead of manufacturer push.

All ninety-eight clients, of course, wanted their copy written by Bruce Barton, and his half-day agreement soon went up in the smoke from his ancient Fox typewriter. By 1923 there was no more room for all the "Bruce Bartons" who were writing copy at 25 West Forty-fifth Street. They found room on the seventh floor of a new building just erected at 383–85 Madison Avenue. At approximately the same minute, the George Batten Company abandoned their location at 371 Fourth Avenue, where they had been since 1910, and moved into the tenth floor, and half of the ninth, in the same building.

The building had just been awarded a prize, probably for humility, but the diploma said, "For the Best New Building of the Year." This may be the first time you have learned that this cube-full of cubes was "Modern Renaissance," or that the entire Madison Avenue side was faced with Indiana Limestone. The tenth-floor ceiling was a foot higher than the other floors. This was because originally a rug merchant, who wanted to display his rugs on end, was to be the occupant. The architects, Cross and Brown, also received diplomas.

The worse thing about being president of an agency is that you are expected to make calls on the clients—not at special meetings where advertising is discussed—but just at any old time to "see how things are going."

Bruce took off for Detroit for a visit with Bill Knudsen, the head of Chevrolet, and later of the War Production Board. Knudsen was a Scandinavian, a blunt man with a low threshold of tolerance for advertising men. He said nothing but "Hello"—so Bruce started off:

"Mr. Knudsen, what is your real opinion of your 1931 Chevrolet?"

Mr. Knudsen pondered the question. "It is almost the perfect car. Ah, but next year! Next year we will have the perfect car!"

"What changes will you make?" asked Bruce, who did not realize that plans for next year's car are as carefully guarded in Detroit as the gold is in Fort Knox, if there is still any there.

"You know about automobiles? You know what is the chassis?"

Bruce, who lived in the city and rented a car when he needed one, said he did know what the chassis was.

"Well on each corner of the chassis we are putting little hooks."

"And what are the hooks for?"

"From these hooks we are hanging a canvas, like it was a hammock."

"And what will that do, Mr. Knudsen?"

"Catch all the goddam parts that fall out!"

A couple of Yale boys dropped in to see Bruce Barton in 1924. They had been referred to Bruce by Dwight Morrow, then ambassador to Mexico. He knew that Bruce had once been an editor and thought he might be able to advise the boys, who were planning a magazine.

"First of all," said Bruce, "you must have a minimum of half a million dollars that you can afford to lose—a million would be better."

"We have been able to raise only $280,000, but we think we'll try anyway," said Henry Luce and Briton Hadden.

---

A self-made man, and proud of it, still managed to keep his sense of humor. He was asked, "What is the secret of your success?"

To which he replied, "My good judgment."

"What gave you your good judgment?"

"Experience."

"And what gave you your experience?"

"My bad judgment."

*There's an advertising agency*
  *Whose name really grooves*
*Its name has got a beat*
  *A beat that I can't lose*
*I've got those Batten, Barton, Dur-*
  *stine & Osborn blues.*

*Well, Benton may have his Bowles,*
  *And Sullivan his three souls*
*Ogilvy has his pair*
  *And N.W.'s got his Ayer*
*But there's four names I can never*
  *lose*
    *I've got those Batten, Barton, Dur-*
    *stine & Osborn blues.*

*McCann's got Erickson*
  *And Ruthrauff's got Ryan*
*Walter Thompson has his "J"*
  *But I've got those blues I never*
  *lose*
*I've got those Batten, Barton, Dur-*
  *stine & Osborn blues.*

OLD FOLK SONG

# The Merger

## 10

☞ The Batten Company merged with Barton, Durstine and Osborn three months after hiring me. I have as yet been unable to find any causative relationship between these two events. Bill Benton said he got fired for suggesting the merger. Papa Johns claimed that *he* started it by mentioning slyly to Roy Durstine, coming up in the elevator, "Roy, did it ever occur to you that we have no competitive accounts? Think it over." And placing his finger beside his nose, up the elevator he rose, still smiling conspiratorially as he hopped off at the tenth.

The union had not yet permitted an extension of the office grapevine into my cubbyhole. So I heard not a whisper about merger.

Then I was invited to come right into Mr. Johns's office. Batten men lined the walls. I pursued my little personal game of wondering which of them was the account executive on the National Casket account. They mostly looked the part.

One man was a stranger. He was medium in height. In fact he looked very much like a retired lightweight fighter who had led too often with his chin. Hands in pockets, he rocked back and forth like a man who has a chore to do, and wishes to do it right now so he can get on with more important things.

"I want you all to meet one of our new partners, Roy Durstine," Mr. Johns said.

There was no great gasp of surprise, since everyone already knew about it but me.

Mr. Durstine made a brief speech. Things were going to be better than ever before for all of us. This was because we had different strengths which, added together, would surely make us the greatest agency in the world. The name temporarily would combine the two agency names. Bruce Barton was thinking up a permanent name. Bruce believed that, since we constantly preached brevity, we ought also to practice it.

Papa Johns would be president of the combine, and Bruce would move up to chairman. As for Roy Durstine, he didn't give a damn for titles and would take any that was handy as long as everyone knew that he ran the place!

Roy was named vice-president and general manager. Today you can become a vice-president by saving up ten merit badges, but the great dilution of titles had not set in yet, and being a vice-president was a great honor. Now we have as many titles as Howard Johnson has flavors. Titles, I have found, are most attractive before you get them. When you get them, you learn a great truth. The fun is not getting the title, but in running the race. Once you've made it, it bursts in your face like a tiny bubble, leaving you with only a slightly damp nose. Titles are great for the little woman back home, however. "You must have heard of my husband, dear. He's vice-president of Turtle, Nurtle and Slogoing."

Bruce Barton's struggle to find a new name for the new agency never had a chance. The long funny name caught on too fast. Fred Allen told them from coast to coast that it sounded like a trunk falling down stairs.

James Cagney in "Hard to Handle" said, "So long, boys. I am having lunch with Batten, Barton, Durstine & Osborn."

Franklin D. Roosevelt attempted to name us "Martin, Barton and Fish."

Harry Truman preferred "Bunko, Bull, Deceit and Obfuscation."

Where does a Batten, Barton, Durstine & Osborn girl go on her vacation? To Baden-Baden, Dresden and Oslo. Where else?

The *New Yorker* reported that a litter of five kittens had been named "Batten," "Barton," "Durstine," "Osborn" and "God."

A jittery father filled out his baby's hospital card naming Batten, Barton, Durstine & Osborn as next of kin.

Jack Benny, on his program for American Tobacco, "phoned" us frequently. The phone girl never failed to reply, "Batten, Barton, Durstine and Little ol' Osborn."

Martin Agronsky told me that, when he was reporting from Singapore during World War II, the usually slow-paced rickshaw men would burst into a fast trot if you yelled, "Batten, Barton, Durstine & Osborn" at them.

Somewhere along the way the ampersand got lost. Now we are mostly known as BBDO. But we answer eagerly to anything. Even to a letter addressed to "Batten Barton Durstine and Schwartz" received a year or so ago.

Mr. Johns had exaggerated just the least bit when he told Roy Durstine that we had no competitive accounts. Wonder Bread and Bond Bread were about as competitive as you can get. We also had Raleigh Smoking Tobacco and Edgeworth. And the only way we hung onto Edgeworth was to have Mr. Johns promise to put every layout, schedule, correspondence, indeed every scrap of paper concerning Edgeworth, in his safe before going home each night.

This fear of being in the same agency as a competitor is an amusing phenomenon. Having the same film or tape producers, having the same typographers, it is very difficult to avoid knowing what the rival company is up to. And the number of "secrets" worth stealing is limited.

Rumors in the newly merged agency became so loud that even I could hear them. Naturally, people were nervous because we had two of almost everything—and you just do not need two chief art directors, two heads of production, or even two treasurers. The rumor mill ground rapidly. BDO had bought Batten just to get their accounts, and all the Batten people would be fired. And the same rumor, reversing the names, ran through the BDO people.

It got so hot that management was moved to issue memos:

Johns: Neither of us has swallowed the other. We have come together on an equal basis. This is an honest effort to improve our service to clients, to strengthen and perpetuate both institutions.

Durstine: Nobody bought anybody else. Mr. Johns' agency is 37 years old. Phases of advertising that we are just studying have become second nature to them. Both organizations are doing famously well.

J. Stirling Getchell, who had left us by then, said: Two one-legged men getting together to walk.

There was more truth in Getchell's wisecrack than in Durstine's statement that "both organizations are doing famously well." BDO got new business fast but, according to probably prejudiced Batten people, was not so good at serving it. Mr. Johns, now a mature 250 pounds and nearing his sixties, was no longer a hound for new business. Indeed, Durstine pretty well sawed him off by giving Johns's responsibilities to others, including himself. Johns sat in his big corner office, behind his big desk, writing answers to form letters and waiting for the phone to ring. We assigned two younger men to new business who had the appropriate names of Eager and Gouge, but even that did not produce any magic.

It is fascinating to realize that the highest annual billing for the old Batten Company was eleven million dollars. With his share of the profit from this billing, Mr. Johns owned the *Welcome,* a seventy-two-foot cruiser, was commodore of the Bayside Yacht Club, had his own chauffeur, and a home in Boca Grande as well as Bayside. Batten and his 400-acre New Jersey cattle ranch near Morristown did equally well. Mr. Johns never took a vacation. He did, indeed, go to Florida regularly, but that was for the company's good. He was able to rest up (for the good of the company) and take a long-range view of things (for the good of the company). Strangely he seemed to need this rest and long-range view in the wintertime. We made bets on when Mr. Johns would leave on his non-vacation. The girl at our ticket —and petty cash—window let us know who won.

The merger just did not seem to take, despite the news that it had been consummated one evening on an art director's desk. Mr. Johns knew what was needed. What was needed was a great big smashing party!

Memo from Mr. Johns:

Yes, there will be a party on January 23rd, 1931 at the Roosevelt. There will be business sessions during the day and a "bigger and better than ever" party for all of us in the evening. In addition to the New Yorkers, a real snappy dance orchestra, you will be treated to a real professional BBDO radio broadcast. Also Vee Lawnhurst and Muriel Pollock (the Lady Bugs). This party is something you won't want to miss.

It was also the last. Several low characters spiked the punch and even flaunted bottles. Venturesome girls, propelled by bottled bravery, tried to climb upon Mr. Johns's lap. Then a snowstorm struck. Mr. Johns announced that there would be rooms available for any woman who did not want to face the storm. Almost every girl was suddenly frightened of snow. Men, too, developed this fear, along with a strong reluctance to stay out of the girls' rooms. The party was everything that Mr. Johns had promised and a lot of other things that had never crossed his mind!

If the merger was supposed to weld Batten's service ability to BDO's new business ability, it did not work out exactly as planned. The first full year of the combined company showed a billing figure of $32.6 million. From there it bumped down the stairs a year at a time for ten years until it hit $17.3 million. Barton decided to be a Congressman. The owners suddenly figured that it was unfair to have so few own stock in the company. It was not exactly a generous gesture. They simply wanted to unload.

Feland, that same old Robley—asked me how many shares I wanted to take. I took all I could, 300 shares. My salary had been cut to $9,000 a year, and the number three child had just joined the family. The stock was to pay for itself out of its dividends.

But I had to contribute five cents a share each payday and 300 nickels is fifteen dollars!

What went wrong? There was the handy excuse of the depression. But mostly it was Roy's theory of the "all-round" advertising man. Roy thought everyone should be able to contact, write copy, specify type, direct a commercial. He thought he could—so why couldn't everyone else? He abolished the copy department, and the art department, and scattered the people concerned throughout the contact groups. The result was thirty little agencies with nothing in common but the toilets. These little agencies in turn reported to three men of adequate incompetence.

It took ten years to discover that the theory was false. A few writers became all-round admen—but they preferred to make ads. No contact man learned to be creative. You cannot learn to write. You can learn to write better. But writing is like the measles—either you catch it or you don't.

Roy refused to hire any radio talent at more than Roy was being paid. Also he would not permit BBDO to have a liquor account, although he was on the friendliest terms with it himself. As a result of this friendship, he sometimes went to the wrong client, at the wrong time, for the wrong meeting. And sometimes he took the wrong people with him. Finally it was decided that Roy, who was about to go through personal bankruptcy, would have to go.

But who could fire him? Only the Executive Committee. Were they mice or men? A landslide for mice! Roy was met by our lawyer, Gene McQuade, in Phoenix, where he was honeymooning with a new wife and a new Cadillac. Once Roy was out, his theories of the all-round adman were dropped. That was 1938, and it took twelve more years to get back to our 1929 billing. By that time I was copy chief, getting paid $15,000 a year.

That doesn't sound like much today, when even kids get $1,000 for every year they have lived. But it looked like a lot to me!

Franklin P. Adams (F.P.A.) aided and abetted a little game which was called "Advertisingitis." The idea was to create some gibberish, containing the name of a well-known store or product. Such as "the Quality of Macy's is not strained" . . . "Forhan's twenty blackbirds" . . . " 'Shoot if Yuban this old gray head but Spearmint country's flag' she said." Don't blame *me,* I'm just the reporter around here!

---

Once, when *The New Yorker* magazine was young and new, we did circulation advertising for it. It was a rather exciting account. One day our account executive, Tax Cumings, found himself alone in the elevator with the great editor, Harold Ross.

"Mr. Ross," Tax said, "do you realize that *The New Yorker* now has 250,000 readers?"

"Indeed?" asked Ross. "And how *are* they all?"

# How to
# almost
# get a raise

## 11

About ten minutes after the merger, Roy Durstine started to move people. The Batten radio department was George Podeyn and Grace Crane Smith. The Barton, Durstine & Osborn radio bureau was somewhat more advanced and it was headed by Arthur Pryor, Junior, son of the famous bandmaster. Durstine moved our little twosome down to the seventh floor because he was more interested in radio than anything else (within the office, that is). So George Podeyn became the first Batten man to "go downstairs."

One morning a rose appeared on Podeyn's desk. Someone asked him what the hell that was for, and George said it was because it was his "Batten Birthday." This amused the BDO kids all to pieces. A dozen of them joined hands and danced around him singing, "Happy Batten Birthday to You."

Ben Duffy used to say that you could put one agency in one

corner of Grand Central Station, and the other agency in the other and you could not tell the difference by looking at them. But there was a difference.

When the two companies moved into 383 Madison Avenue, the Batten Company was thirty-seven years old. George Batten, and Mr. Johns after him, expected and got the respect due their age. Paternalism and tradition ruled the actions of the younger Batten people. BDO, on the other hand, was four years old. Everybody, bosses and employees, were about the same age. Everyone was on a first-name basis. Batten people would never have danced around a BDO man's desk. Why not? Because they would probably have been fired if they did. They envied the free and easy swinging BDO group, but all their background kept them from joining the fun.

Joe Alger, BDO's main cutup, carried a police whistle, which he found handy in restaurants where service lagged. It seemed to speed things up. Joe claimed to be the president of the Anti-Cole-Slaw League of America, and had a card to prove it, which he handed each waitress with his order.

The big thing then at the movies was "Everybody sing! Just follow the bouncing ball!" Joe was not above going directly from lunch to the Paramount if things didn't seem to be too pressing at the office.

New Yorkers, of course, would have none of this hokey bouncing ball, sing-along stuff, and sat in grim silence. All but Joe. He would sing at the top of his voice until finally an usher would tell him to shut up. Joe would then argue loudly that the manager of the theater must want him to sing, or he wouldn't have that message on the screen asking him to.

Joe also destroyed the Batten Birthday and the rose, by sending Papa Johns a little note that read:

*When you gave me a rose*
*Instead of a raise*
*You sure got a rise*
*Out of me!*

Distant thunder was again heard, but no lightning struck. And the roses disappeared.

Jerry Alexander, a gifted mimic, could imitate Mr. Johns's voice so that Mrs. Johns would never have known the difference. One

Saturday afternoon, he stayed in the office and dictated a number of raises on Mr. Johns's dictaphone, addressing them to the company's treasurer. They would unquestionably have gone through except that Mr. Johns's secretary, Edith Powell, knew that Mr. Johns never threw money around that way. There were too many raises, and all were too big. The Johns harr-umphs mounted to the ceiling, but he never found the villain, although anyone else in the agency could have told him.

Polly Adler's pleasure dome was just up the street, and she billed monthly. As far as I know, no Batten man patronized her, but I did get several misdirected bills meant for a BDO man whose name resembled mine. As for me, I was always the "I'll have a drink, but I won't go upstairs" type. I blame this reticence on my mother, who warned me, when I ran away from home at sixteen, to "keep away from those bawdy houses." I thought it was spelled b-o-d-y—and I didn't want to get my fenders bent.

A very revealing glimpse of the BDO frivolity and Batten stuffiness may be seen in the memos of each company announcing the move to 383 Madison Avenue.

Mr. Johns's message to his troops:

When the turmoil is over and we have settled down to work, you will realize, *as you do not now* [italics mine] that this is more than a change of location. It is an important advance in our business history. It marks our faith in the George Batten Company.

From *Sparks*, the BDO house organ:

### BDO MOVES INTO SPACE
### MORE SPACIOUS AND GRACIOUS!

New concrete stadium at 383 Madison Avenue has seating capacity for double attendance at the big game. "BDO shift greatest migration since Exodus" says Mayor Hylan. "A short step across, a big step ahead," says Tom Ryan.

Tom Ryan made the step forward a bit shorter by escaping with the Ipana account and setting up a new agency, Pedlar and Ryan.

At that time I knew little about our rival agency downstairs. We played baseball against them and sang our alma mater, "Batten Will Shine Tonight." I was far too busy serving my sentence on Wonder Bread.

Either through loyalty or inertia, and you had better bet it was inertia, I worked for eight years on that loaf of bread, until Ted Bates resigned and took it along to Benton and Bowles—where he parked long enough to latch onto Colgate and, with the two accounts, set up his own agency.

I read Ted's obit while writing this. If he went to heaven—and he would have rejected anything less—things are going to be different up yonder.

My start on the Wonder Bread account was inauspicious—due to my opening my large and witty mouth. I was introduced to the sales manager, George Godfried. He had once given his old tuxedo to the boy next door, who gave it to me.

"I believe we are related through a mutual tuxedo," I said. He didn't seem to understand, so I went into details, while everyone else developed a sudden interest in looking at the floor.

After I left the room, Mr. Godfried suggested that I be thrown to the lions, dropped out of the tenth-floor window, hanged, quartered and drawn or otherwise disposed of. He was damned if he was going to pay 15 per cent of four million dollars for the services of a ragamuffin who couldn't even afford a new tux.

Since we had no one else at the moment I was kept on the account, but away from Mr. Godfried. This was not difficult, because there were around thirty Wonder Bakers in thirty Wonder Bakeries (all singing, "Yoho! Yoho! Yoho ahead, we are the bakers of Wonder Bread," etc.) and each had his own local problems. So most of my time was spent on the road. One time I was out for six weeks, and when I knocked on the front door, my three-year-old son yelled upstairs to his mother, "Mommy! Daddy came over!"

At college (pre-inflation) we often discussed our hopes for an adequate income. We agreed that a hundred dollars a week would be just great. But it took me years to get there. I couldn't seem to get a raise, just because others were getting cuts. Each year the company issued new desk calendars. I would immediately turn to the following December 31—and write down all the dire things I would cause to happen if I had no raise by then.

It wasn't that I didn't ask. I never got a raise without asking until I was made executive vice-president. On that glad day I got messages of congratulation from the management, and a note from Dorothy Lawrence, our money girl, that my paycheck was held up until I caught up on my expense accounts.

When I asked for a raise, my "best friend" the treasurer, Robley Feland, would chide me gently by saying, "Hell no, and stop bothering me." I related the thing about the squeaking wheel gets the grease. He said, "Did I ever tell you about the farmer who got so tired of listening to that squeak that he threw the whole damned wheel away?" That frightened me into silence for a whole month.

I really needed money. My bootleg script business had long ago folded. There was a girl out in Pasadena named Elizabeth. I wrote the "bridges" between the Wonder Bakers songs. Whenever the song was appropriate, such as "I Love You Truly," I would write, "The next song is dedicated to our little friend in Pasadena"; then I would rush a telegram West saying be sure to tune in KECA tonight.

Like all good rackets, this one came to an end. Mr. Godfried, who occasionally listened to his own program, blew slightly up.

"What's all the 'Little friend in Pasadena' stuff?" he roared inquiringly. "Why, Goddammit, we don't even have a bakery there!"

Eventually we lost Wonder Bread, but won Elizabeth. She's around here somewhere now wondering if I am ever going to learn to put my shoes away. Since the wedding was forty-three years ago, it seems unlikely that I will learn anything much.

By this time I was also working on Armstrong. They make millions of things beside resilient floors. My favorite product at that time was "Hot Bottom Filler" (also Cold); it's the stuff that goes between the outer sole and innersole of your shoe.

They knew that I was heading to Pasadena and marriage. But they also knew that the Pennsylvania Limited stopped at Lancaster. All I had to do was to start West a day sooner. When you are in the advertising business you can't turn down logic like that.

Eventually I got the hundred dollars a week. I was by then a copy group head, with four writers under me. One of them was a lady that someone had met at a bar. She was getting $1,300 a year more than I was, and the only thing she wrote real well was her name when endorsing a paycheck. Managements are odd, that way. They actually believe that salaries are secret.

I consoled myself with the thought that some elder statesman had given me . . . "In this business you are underpaid for the first half of your career, and overpaid for the second." He was right, and overpaid is better.

Phrases from the "Jazz Age" now (1933) definitely dead:

| | | |
|---|---|---|
| Atta boy | Flat tire | *Make passes |
| Atta girl | *Flop | Oh, yeah |
| And how | *Gyp | Pash |
| *Be yourself | *Have a heart | Poor fish |
| *Big shot | High hat | Simp |
| Blotto | *Hokum | *Step on it |
| Boob | Hot spot | Sugar daddy |
| *Boy friend | Love nest | Up and up |

Still going strong (1933) but will probably wear out soon:

| | | |
|---|---|---|
| *Can't take it | *Scram | Old hat |
| *Fold up | So what? | Swish |
| *Racket | You' telling me | Dope |
| Pay-off | Heavy muffin | Swank |
| *On the spot | Die on the vine | Crush party |
| On the make | *Gadget | No sale |

*Asterisks indicate words and phrases that have not died, but have moved into common usage and are no longer considered slang. Any, asterisked or unasterisked, seem to be superior to "That's the name of the game," or "That's for sure," or "You really know how to hurt a guy" or even "Right on!"

# The graduate
# of Churchill
# Downs

## 12

☞ He gave his wife a compost heap for Christmas—and another year a fistful of Raleigh coupons. He told his small brood of children that Christmas was a Catholic holiday, and not for them. He did gather them about him at Christmastime and read them Dickens' "A Christmas Carol" . . . but only to the place where Scrooge says, "Bah . . . Humbug." And many years later, when a daughter had children of her own, he sent her a check for twenty-five dollars "to help the children celebrate the glorious Yuletide and the birthday of our blessed Lord and Saviour whose name for the moment escapes me." He disliked women in general and maintained that they attracted moths—pointing out that moths are never found in men's clubs. But he liked one of them enough to have six children—the fifth of whom he named Quintus Ultimus. This son was permitted to drop the Ultimus, when a younger brother was born.

Robley was a nickname, conferred upon Faris Robison Feland to honor either him or Robley ("Fighting Bob") Evans, a hero of the Spanish American war. Back home he was known as "Rob." The folks down in Kentucky had a simple way of remembering his birthday after he came North. They named one of their cows Rob's Birthday and thus were constantly reminded.

Robley's start was inauspicious. He was saved from graduating at the foot of his high school class by his friend Clarence Wood, who got 64.51 to Robley's 64.55. He became a double dropout at the University of Kentucky, and wrote on his Batten application blank under *Education:* "Continuous, interrupted only by two years of college." His children said, "Father graduated from Churchill Downs."

For some time he hung around town, sampling the local Bourbon and working intermittently on his father's newspaper. Had his father not been "The Judge," his son might have been called a bum. As it was, he was described as "triflin'." His father, unsympathetic to the pleasures of doing nothing, bundled him off to East Aurora, New York, where Elbert Hubbard, who liked to be known as Fra Elbertus, ran a press, published a magazine, *The Philistine,* which was printed on butcher paper, and invited the Great and Near Great to East Aurora. They came in droves, as did young people from all parts of the country, which was somewhat difficult in those pre-hitchhiking days.

According to Robley, Hubbard invented the word kabojalism, which was the opposite of plagiarism. You thought up something great and attributed it to someone great, so that people might pay more attention to it. Again, according to Robley, over the door of the great hall in East Aurora was carved the whole better-mouse-trap business credited to Ralph Waldo Emerson—but actually written by Fra Elbertus.

Hubbard's magazine took advertising, but it had to be written by the Fra. Advertising agencies could send in whatever copy they liked—but it would be rewritten by Hubbard or some of his many assistants. Robley graduated from mowing the lawn and became one of these assistants. Then, having married, he took off for New York, spent a disastrous two weeks with the old Federal Agency and somehow got himself hired by George Batten.

I was not around here when in 1910 Robley blew in on a brisk March breeze, so I must accept the word of others that "He looked like a freak." Actually he was dressed in perfect imitation of Hubbard—black overcoat from chin to sidewalk, black hat the size of a small buggy wheel, and a flowing black tie, big enough to hide anything that might otherwise remain visible. Someone rushed him to a tailor, and he wore tailored suits thereafter, although they looked as though he had walked around while being measured. There were secret pockets, too, for his racetrack winnings.

When I first knew him, people were asking for his autograph. They thought he was W. C. Fields. Alone with him in an elevator a girl asked the same old question.

"No," he said, "I'm not W. C. Fields. But I will tell you who I really am if you want to know." She did.

"I'm God!"

His real estimate of himself fell short of that claim.

"I like to buy a man a drink or win money from him, but the strong hearty handclasp, the full look in the eye, the encouraging slap on the shoulder, the booming 'Get in there and win, old man —you've got it in you!' are not in my bag of tricks."

Despite this handicap, Mr. Johns was delighted with him and nine years after he was hired, Robley was head of the copy department, with a rumored ten ads in a single copy of *The Saturday Evening Post*. But as copy chief he was a disaster. He seemed unable to hire or fire anyone. If he did not like a man's work, he would simply glare at him, and give him no more assignments. In desperation Mr. Johns brought William Boardman down from Batten's Boston office and made him "creative head" over both copy and art, and thus over Robley.

The story that Robley went home to Nutley, N.J., and stayed in bed three days until a delegation of Batten executives came out to New Jersey and pleaded with him to return is probably untrue, but in character. Roy Durstine tried to make an account executive out of him (he had really brought in the Wonder Bread account, mostly because the sales manager was his next door neighbor). Alas, Robley was no better at contact than he was as copy chief. Roy Durstine wanted to fire him, but there was not enough money around to buy his stock.

So, naturally enough, he had him made treasurer. What better qualifications can a treasurer have than a taste for Bourbon and an addiction to horses?

As Robley was leaving the directors meeting that had elected him treasurer, Mr. Johns motioned for him to come into his office.

"I need some sound financial advice."

"My God," groaned Robley. "An hour ago I was a copywriter trying to be an account executive. Just because they elect me treasurer you expect me to be instantly filled with financial wisdom?"

Meanwhile Robley had made a discovery that would save him from hard work the rest of his prosperous life. Wandering through the offices, he saw no bookshelves. Visiting friends in advertising, he found no collections of books. It was apparent to him that advertising agency people did not read much. Trade papers, mainly. But never Sir Francis Bacon, Aristotle, La Rochefoucauld, Schopenhauer or even Shakespeare. Robley read all of these— underlined especially memorable thoughts—and stored them away until the appropriate time came in a meeting. Then he would mumble a fitting quote without the quotes. He became the sage of BBDO. Everyone quoted "Felandisms." He was promoted to the Executive Committee. No important decisions were made without consulting him.

I quote from a letter to a friend: "A very great man named Feland who flourished and drank deep circa the early decades of the 20th Century used to have a saying (which he stole from earlier philosophers, but which he used with impunity on all who knew no philosophers, early or late) which went something like this: 'Never apologize. Your friends do not require it and your enemies will not believe it.' "

This borrowed wisdom, presented with authority, made him a rather rich millionaire.

To be invited into Robley's office for a pre-lunch drink was a sign that you were marked for success, although I do not recall a single case of his actually doing something for anyone. He kept pure bonded Bourbon in his safe, along with a thousand-dollar emergency fund for the horses. There was also a revolver which he had got because someone bet him he couldn't—and now he had no idea of what to do with it. His right-hand desk drawer was filled with corks and his left with carefully folded cellophane from cigarette packs. ("You never know when someone will come along in need of some cellophane and I want to be ready.")

All this, I suspect, was to build his reputation as a character. Robley would pour bonded Bourbon into an old-fashioned glass "right up to the top of the church windows" and hand it to you. No ice, no water. No anything. You either drank it or died trying. When I brought my new wife in to meet him he poured her what was probably her first drink. Tears ran down her cheeks, but he just smiled and smiled, and offered her a second round. She was still able to shake her head.

A young man whose name I have practiced forgetting heard about this drink-with-Robley business and decided to break down the barrier and establish himself at once.

He strode into Feland's office and addressed him as "Robley," which should have brought the building down, but didn't.

"I feel a cold coming on," said our eager friend. "I wonder if you'd mind pouring me a drink?"

Robley was filled with sympathy.

"Not only will I pour you a drink, young man, but I will have it delivered to your office!"

After a couple blasts of Bourbon, Robley would ask where you would like to eat lunch. The only correct answer was "Billy's," because you were going to go there anyway. "Billy-the-Oysterman" had, at that time, a branch on Forty-seventh Street west of Fifth. He also had a crushing handshake and a voice that made the dishes dance on their tables.

"Good morning, Colonel," he would roar at Feland. "I've saved your table for you!" It didn't seem to bother Robley that "your table" was hardly ever the same table. The floors were tile, the chairs rackety and the waiters did not share Billy's enthusiasm. The sole decoration was a huge three-dimensional Lobster with an inscription suggesting that you would have done better had you gone to Hackney's in Atlantic City.

Robley took care of the coat check girl for all of us. He gave her a dime and watched closely to see that she got no more. She was a pretty brunette in her late twenties, whose name, as far as Robley was concerned, was "Miss." Our shame was great and so was our curiosity. For the girl was not only happy with the dime, she sewed on loose buttons and loops on his overcoat.

"A dime is enough," Robley would growl. "She gets a salary and her tips all go to gangsters." This, our research department reported, was not true. Indeed, she was a widow with one child and needed every penny she could get.

Like all criminals, Robley bragged once too often. He told

Lester Cudahay, a friend at The Players, that he considered it part of his job to teach young squirts economy and that you can get perfect service for a dime if you act as though you expected it. To insure his demonstration from failure, however, he sometimes went to lunch alone. On such occasions he gave her five dollars.

I can remember only one decision that Robley ever made, and made it stick. We used to present a new father, but in those days of male chauvinism not a new mother, with a check for a hundred dollars, which, after all the deductions, might buy a can of baby powder.

There came a case where the baby lived only a few hours. Should the father get a check for such a baby?

"I suggest we apply the rule they use down in Kentucky," he said. "If the foal can stand and suck it is considered to have been born alive."

Robley was a self-appointed defender of the English language as it is, was, and ever shall be. He hated the word "contact" used as a verb. Insisted that the word "cushion" was never meant to replace "reserves." The use of "shambles" to describe a disordered room or a wrecked taxi was almost as bad as the use of "decimate" in place of "exterminate."

I did not go along with this pedantry and argued that the English language is a growing thing, and that "common usage" is not a filthy phrase. I rather sided with Henry Ward Beecher, "When grammar gets in my way, so much the worse for grammar!"

Robley was long dead when we wrote "Us Tareyton Smokers would rather fight than switch." The kind of man who would fight over a brand of cigarettes, we figured, would consider "We Tareyton Smokers" a bit effete.

By Pearl Harbor time, Robley and I were fast friends, although I'll never know why. In all the years back and ahead he never did one damned thing for me. People hired much later than I were made stockholders. I was getting less salary than some of my assistants. He could have fixed all this by raising a finger. I suspect he had a heavy finger.

As far as I can remember, he only gave me two pieces of advice. The first was after I had been there only a year. It was a kindly suggestion that I get out of the advertising business. He felt that I was too soft-boiled, not rough and tough enough for this dog-eat-dog business. I told him that being tough was very simple if that was what he wanted—spat in his wastebasket and went out, looking for a dog to eat.

Mostly I succeeded in being tough. But several people saw through the act. One of them was a pretty secretary, who put too much soda in her drinks and got somewhat bubbly at a going-away party for another secretary. Swaying and listing a bit, she grabbed me by the lapels and said:

"Mr. Brower, I don't believe you are mean and tough like they say, at all. I think you are very nice!"

"Now, you listen here," I said. "I have spent forty years building up this bad reputation—and no little secretary is going to ruin it now. Go play somewhere else."

The other piece of advice Robley gave me was in Memorial Hospital, where cancer was ending his days. He was allowed to have all the whiskey he needed, and his visitors could help themselves. The advice: "Charlie, if you don't put the cork back after each drink, you will waste a whole bottleful during your life from evaporation."

In 1942, it looked for a while as though he might have to make a decision. Our copy chief, Les Pearl, had left for the wars. Pearl was an excellent copy chief, but not quite the genius that management had pictured to clients and prospects. When he left, clients said, "What are you going to do now? There's nobody else that could run that department!" As is the custom with many managements, they did nothing except to announce that no one was to occupy Les's office. (I was finally able to move some research files in there—very temporarily.) Finally three of us group heads set up our own troika. But it didn't work any better than it does in Russia. It was like having three directors for one orchestra. Now that I was tough and had survived many skirmishes, I went with what I thought was a determined look to see my old friend Robley.

"A copy department cannot operate without a head," I said. "If the management hasn't the guts to appoint a new copy chief, why not call the copy department together and *elect* one?"

"What good would that do? They would just elect you!"

I ran up the stairs two at a time, and into Alex Osborn's office, where I resigned with assorted dramatic gestures and several words that have since become literature.

The next day I was copy chief.

I believe that Robley was pleased, as long as he was not the responsible one if I fell on my face. The quality of our work seemed not to suffer. Clients began to accept me for what I was —young enough to be eager, old enough to avoid obvious foolishness and a fairly good department head.

It is no easy thing to be the right age in the advertising agency business. The last time I looked, only 15 per cent of us were over forty and only 5 per cent over fifty.

But you might use Robley's trick of becoming a sage, and getting quite rich as you become elderly by stealing from earlier philosophers and using their sayings as your own on all who know no philosophers. In fact I am going to help you with some usable quotes.

**Let us suppose the subject is creativity:**

*To argue or refute*
*Wise councellors abound*
*The man to execute*
*Is harder to be found*
                *La Fontaine*


*Blot out, correct, insert, refine*
*Enlarge, diminish, interline*
*Be mindful when invention fails*
*To scratch your head and bite your nails.*
                *Jonathan Swift*


A powerful agent is the right word. Whenever we come upon one of these intensely right words, in a book or newspaper, the effect is physical as well as spiritual and electrifyingly prompt!
                *Mark Twain*


It is easier to write ten passable sonnets, good enough to take in the not too inquiring critic, than one effective ad-

vertisement that will take in a few thousand of the uncritical buying public.
*Aldous Huxley*

The two most engaging things about a writer are to make new things familiar and familiar things new.
*Thackeray*

**Suppose they keep telling you "this is a young man's business":**

Ideas are like beards, men do not have them until they grow up. *Voltaire*

**When the question of being original comes up, you have at least these three authorities:**

It is as difficult to appropriate the thoughts of others as to invent! *Emerson*

If you want to have a baby, have a *new* one.
*Jessamyn West*

Don't keep forever on the public road going only where others have gone. Leave the beaten path occasionally and dive into the woods. You will be certain to find something that you have never seen before. It will be a little thing but do not ignore it. Follow up. Explore around it, one discovery will lead to another and before you know it, you will have something really worth thinking about. All really big discoveries are the result of thought.
*Alexander Graham Bell*

**Decisions, decisions?**

When I wrote "Pilgrims Progress" some said "John, Print it!" Others said "Not so!" Some said "It may do good." Others said "No." *John Bunyan*

**Excellence is discussed more than it is practiced these days, but you never know when a good quote on the subject might come in handy:**

Quality is never an accident, it is always the result of intelligent effort. There must be the will to produce a superior thing!   *John Ruskin*

Far better it is to dare mighty things and win glorious triumphs, even though checkered by failure, than to take rank among those poor spirits who neither enjoy much nor suffer much, because they live in that gray twilight that knows not victory nor defeat.
*Theodore Roosevelt*

**Are you being underpaid?**

Nobody but a blockhead ever wrote for anything but money.   *Samuel Johnson*

**And here we have a few good lines for account executives:**

One machine can do the work of fifty ordinary men, but no machine can do the work of one extraordinary man.
*Elbert Hubbard*

Attacking is the only secret. Dare and the world always yields. Or, if it doesn't, dare again and it will succumb.
*Thackeray*

You might as well fall on your face as to lean too far over backward.   *James Thurber*

There is endless benefit in knowing when to have done.
*Thomas Carlyle*

**On truth in advertising:**

An honest business never blush to tell.
*Homer*

I read only one newspaper and that more for its advertisements than for its news. Advertisements contain the only truths to be relied upon in a newspaper.

*Thomas Jefferson*

**Is the subject "attacks on advertising"?**

The philosopher and lover of man have much harm to say about trade. But the historian will see that trade was the principal of liberty . . . trade planted America and destroyed feudalism . . . trade makes peace and keeps peace.

*Ralph Waldo Emerson*

**What about humor in advertising?**

The desire for being clever often prevents us from becoming so.

*La Rochefoucauld*

**A lot has been said about statistics—but here's one, new and usable:**

Last year statistics showed that freight car loadings were up while alcoholism was down. Which only shows that more freight cars were getting loaded than people.

*Anonymous*

**On the subject of luck:**

I am a great believer in luck and I find that the harder I work the more I have of it.

*Stephen Leacock*

If you want to get covered with manure, you have to be there when the spreader goes by.

*Charles Brower*

I would rather hire a lucky man than a smart man any day.

*Bruce Barton*

**Is "work" the only dirty four-letter word left in our language?**

Work is never work unless there is something you would rather be doing.
            *Sir James Barrie*

The life of every man is a diary in which he means to write one story and writes another. And his humblest hour is when he compares the volume as it is with what he had vowed to make it.
            *Sir James again*

**As for simplicity, an adman's most valuable discovery:**

Simplify! Simplify! Our life is frittered away by detail.
            *Henry David Thoreau*

To a man who thought he ought to have an increase in salary because a client had told him that he was a greater asset than Bruce Barton, Robley said:

"Suppose we stood you and Mr. Barton up against a wall, gave every stockholder a rifle, and told them they would have to shoot one of you, who do you think would get shot?" The man seemed to know.

---

Short note from Robley Feland to a writer in another agency who accused Robley of stealing his stuff:

Dear Pot,

Yes, I am black.

Kettle

---

Paragraph from a letter by Robley to Mr. Johns, who was in Florida resting up for the good of the company:

"The Newsletter was hoaxed this week. It carried an item saying that Doc Wilson and Arnold Brown planned to leave for Lebigots, N.C., on February 12th. Lebigot's is a French speakeasy on 50th Street, and N.C. stands for "No Credit," a featured sign in that very comfortable and homelike establishment.

# The
# hand-lettering
# on the wall

---

## 13

☞ Behind Robley Feland's graying head, framed and hung on the wall, was this bit of wisdom, stolen from a Greek:

"YOU" said Demosthenes to his great rival orator Aeschines "MAKE THEM SAY 'HOW WELL HE SPEAKS' I MAKE THEM SAY 'LET US MARCH AGAINST PHILIP'"

This was not put on Robley's wall just to prove that Demosthenes was a conceited bore. It presented the advertising philosophy of the times.

It meant that advertisements and commercials that people admire will not move them to action in the marketplace. It meant that quality and action do not go together.

In the thirties and early forties we were taught to appeal to "the twelve-year-old intelligence."

"But," I asked, "wasn't twelve the exact age of Jesus when he confounded the elders in the temple with his wisdom? Some kids are plenty smart at twelve."

They wanted to know what the hell Jesus had to do with advertising. Copy supervisors told us to take our ads back and "dumb them up" . . . write for the people who move their lips when they read!

One of my clients told me, "If you ever feel proud of an ad you have written, if you feel like taking it home to show your wife, tear it up quick and start over. It will be way over the heads of the public."

Bruce had a photographic mural, covering the entire north wall of his office, showing the sweaty and unshirted crowds on the boardwalk at Coney Island, just to keep himself reminded to whom he was writing. Ironically on another wall hung a quotation from Oliver Cromwell's letter to the Church of Scotland: "I beseech you, in the bowels of Christ, think it possible you may be mistaken."

But Bruce never looked down on people, or dumbed up anything. He knew that great writing is at once understandable by the low IQ's, and inspirational to geniuses.

March against Philip? Every great orator from Patrick Henry to Winston Churchill has made them say both, "How well he speaks!" and, "Let us march against Philip." And there is no recorded instance of people saying, "How lousy he speaks—let us march against Philip!"

Here are some of the things in advertising that turn people off, so they do no marching whatever:

Talking like a pitchman instead of like a friend

Not knowing when to shut up

Using too many sales points so they remember none

Talking about the product instead of what it will do for the reader or listener

Being too important about a product of small importance

Being too urgent . . . too Hurry! Hurry! Hurry

Making unbelievable and unsupported claims

Being confusing

Making the reader or listener work to get your message

Being just plain silly

Worst of all—being dull

*Conversely, people are turned on to your advertising by:*

Friendly help—but not too friendly. Nobody wants you to wag your tail or jump up to lick his hand

Simplicity (consider that as written ten times over)

Wit, but not clowning

Real news, but not fake news

Advertisements that reward reading or listening

A logical development of a single idea

Service suggestion (how to use)

New uses for familiar products

Interest, even borrowed interest

It seems to me that the advertiser, when he asks someone to read his advertisement or listen to his commercial, agrees to an unwritten contract: "If you will spend part of your life with me, even though it be but a few seconds, I in turn will reward you. I will send you away with some bit of new information, however small, some degree of entertainment, be it ever so slight, some feeling of satisfaction that you did not have before."

The two greatest reasons for advertising mediocrity are, mediocre writers and client assistance. When Les Pearl was with us he wrote copy for Hart, Schaffner and Marx, and also for the stores they owned—Wallachs. The president of HS&M asked Les why he always gave the stores better copy than the parent company. Les explained that he got too much help from the president of the parent company—and none whatever from the man in charge of stores.

I am not scorning client control. I believe that most clients are brighter than agency men. A lot more of them are graduates of notable business schools. I am only saying—the agency writer is trained in his trade. Why should clients do his work for him? Just tell him clearly and honestly what you dislike, and let him go away and change it. If you think the writers on your account are not good enough, make the agency change them.

The one ingredient a writer needs is enthusiasm. He has to get himself worked up, even if he is writing about safety pins. I have had writers come in to me and ask, "How do you want this ad—sweet, tough, loud, soft or what? I can write it any way you like!" In such cases I have reassigned the job and eventually reassigned the writer. If a writer is excited and interested, he cannot help writing well. Here is a piece of copy written by a truck driver—or rather dictated to the United Press reporter. You can tell that the reporter wisely never changed a word.

My wife, June, was in labor in the delivery room at St. Anthony's Hospital when it caught fire.

She kicked the screen out of the window and climbed down a ladder against a roof on the second floor. I watched her come down.

Then we took her home. At 1:30 A.M. today she had a boy. He's our third child. My wife's a blue-eyed blonde, 25.

She told me we ought to name the new baby "Lucky."

She was the bravest thing I ever saw.

I was home asleep about midnight when I heard the hospital was on fire. I ran three blocks to the hospital.

When I arrived someone was pushing at the screen on the delivery room window just above the roof. It was June.

Flames and smoke were shooting all around. The firemen put the ladder up there.

June knocked the screen out and crawled onto the roof. Then she started down the ladder. I didn't dare try to go up after her.

I was afraid for her. I didn't know what was going to happen. But she got down. I was there waiting for her. I took her to someone's house across the street.

Then we took her home. The boy was born about an hour

after we got there. The doctor came in to see her. He was there when the baby was born.

I have carried this clipping around with me since 1949. Bruce Barton favors the Lord's Prayer, and Lincoln's Gettysburg Address as examples of clear, simple writing.

Me? I'll take Mr. Arnold Aderman, truck driver, of Effingham, Illinois!

Letter from Tom Dillon, president of BBDO, but in July 1943 copy chief of the San Francisco office:

All my life I have wanted to be a gripman on a cable car.

"Look," I said to the man at the cobwebbed desk, "I wondered if I could do a little part time work. The man got up to block my possible escape.

"Young man, we are forty men short on this line. If you don't help us out. . . ."

After two weeks, I have learned: Whatever happens, you make your "let go," which means that you let go of the cable when you come to the place where it goes into the power house. If you don't, you send yourself and all your passengers through the front window, close down the line for a day and cost the company a minimum of $4000. Next week I expect to run a car of my own.

Tom was transferred with suspicious suddenness to office work. Did he cut a cable? Ask him someday, I'm afraid to.

# He had
# a little
# list

## 14

☞ The pen may be mightier than the sword, but the needle is mightiest of all! The following list was found in the drawer of an abandoned file cabinet along with the bones of the author who compiled it nearly fifty years ago. I repeat it here, mainly to show how things have improved . . .

> *A list of client remarks and*
> *queries guaranteed to produce*
> *premature grayness, arterio-sclerosis*
> *and a cynical outlook on life*

Why do you write such long copy? People haven't time to read long copy anymore.

I don't get it. And if *I* don't get it, there'll be a lot of other people who don't get it either.

My wife looked through the magazine last night and never saw our ad. How do you account for that?

Why do you recommend the *Post?* Does Mr. Curtis need another yacht?

Magazines are getting so thick these days that even a double spread is lost in them. What's the limit to this sort of thing?

Why can't you fellows get up an idea like Halitosis?

Since radio came in, people don't read anymore.

Do you honestly think anybody is going to read this stuff?

This may be your idea of a pretty girl, but it sure isn't mine.

Three weeks! I know a firm in St. Louis that will make a dandy set of plates in three days!

Excuse me while I ask my secretary whether this model looks like a lady or not.

A hundred and fifty dollars for a piece of artwork! I know a girl who is studying art here in town who'll do it for fifteen, maybe ten.

I think the public is getting tired of pretty girls.

Flash from our Chicago office, June 11, 1930:

Last night came the shocking news that Cracker Jack was not being sold at the Ball Park of the Chicago Cubs. Bud Palmer wrote an open letter to William Wrigley in the form of a full page newspaper ad addressed to "Dear Bill." It pointed out that the reason the Cubs were losing all their games was "no Cracker Jack in the Park." The Cubs had cracker-jack batters, cracker-jack pitchers, a cracker-jack outfield, but no Cracker Jack. After overcoming some fear of reprisal, the client consented. Monday afternoon when the ad appeared more Cracker Jack was sold in the vicinity of Wrigley Field than ever before. Seventy-five stores near the field displayed big signs, "Buy Cracker Jack here! Help the Cubs win. Not only that but the Cubs started winning a game here and there. Isn't advertising wonderful?

# *All the weasels died*

## 15

☞ When Theodore Roosevelt, "The Trust Buster," attempted to bust some forty-three trusts during his term in office, he didn't quite make it. One trust that was left over was broken up by the Supreme Court (May 11, 1911). This trust owned nearly every tobacco-processing company in the United States, plus companies that made machinery for the manufacturers. Altogether it sold 90 per cent of all tobacco sold in this country, and much that was sold abroad.

The individual companies that were freed from the trust are mostly familiar today. American Tobacco (now American Brands), Lorillard (oldest of them all), R. J. Reynolds and Liggett and Myers.

The British-American Tobacco Company was the unit that exported all the brands in the trust. The Supreme Court's decision did not strip them of this right. Hence the Luckies you

smoke abroad are made in America, not by the American To-
bacco Company, which makes and sells them in the United
States, but by a subsidiary of the British-American Company in
Louisville. Also, there was nothing in the decree to keep British-
American from selling their own brands here. Naturally, James
Buchanan "Buck" Duke, who had headed the trust, chose as his
company British-American.

Cigarettes were a rather piddling part of tobacco sales in 1911.
Chewing tobacco was far more important. So were smoking tobacco and cigars. Although the Bonsack cigarette machine had
been invented in 1883, most cigarette smokers still preferred to
roll their own, and the type of cigarettes we know today were
dubbed "tailor-made."

The end of the trust meant the beginning of competition.
Liggett and Myers decided to push Fatima—a cigarette with a
high content of aromatic Turkish tobacco. Fatima's slogan, "What
a whale of a difference a few cents makes," was only too true.
People just did not have those few cents. Then the war shut off
the import of Turkish and Egyptian tobaccos, and Liggett and
Myers put their advertising behind Chesterfield. American Tobacco decided to ride along with Sweet Caporal ("Ask Dad, he
knows"). But apparently the thought of Dad was as counter-
productive then as now. The unblended Virginia Bright tobacco
did not hit the spot with U.S. tastes, and American brought out
a new cigarette, named after one of their smoking tobaccos:
Lucky Strike. R. J. Reynolds himself was very much alive then,
and he had an idea. Burley tobacco is cheaper than Virginia
Bright. By mixing the two and adding rum and other flavors he
created the kind of cigarette that Americans love and British dislike today. Furthermore, because Burley tobacco was less expensive, he could sell a pack for ten cents, where most of his
competitors were getting fifteen. As for a name—there was none
of this scientific selection that picks the right name from thousands, as we do today. Barnum and Bailey's Circus was in
Winston with Old Joe, a dromedary. So the new cigarette was
named Camel. Because it suited American tastes, and was not
handicapped by the lack of Egyptian and Turkish, Camel took
off and led the other brands for decades.

Meanwhile British-American was not about to stay out of the
world's best cigarette market and in 1927 they bought Brown and

Williamson, a plug and snuff producer then located in Winston. By the time I got around to hearing about them, they were somewhat bigger, located in Louisville, and their Sir Walter Raleigh Smoking Tobacco came with us when we merged with their agency, BDO. It may not be the best of taste to talk about the "good old days" when you are in the midst of much better days, but I am sure that American Brands knows of this one small wild oat sowed in our youth and forgives us for it.

Among the things we gave Brown and Williamson was the name Kool and a penguin to go with it. The ad manager of B&W was not a penguin type. "Have you ever been in a pen with penguins?" "No." "Have you ever smelled penguin shit?" We admitted our penguinal ignorance, but one thing we did have: a straw vote on what *people* thought of penguins. People thought penguins were cute as hell, with their twisty walk and their formal dress. Eventually "Willy," as the penguin became known, waddled over to Bates, where they boiled and ate him.

I never met Sir Hugo Cunliffe Owen and I don't know anyone who has. But it seems to me that he came to America once each year to see how his British-American subsidiary was making out.

In England they were putting filters on their cigarettes. Not for any purpose of filtration, you understand, but just to keep bits of tobacco from sticking to your lips. It happened that Sir Hugo had one too many filter machines over there. Why shouldn't Brown and Williamson take the machine and see if filters might not go in the United States as they had in the United Kingdom?

The machine arrived, was installed, and began to spew out filter cigarettes. Where the name Viceroy came from I do not know but through some oversight we were appointed as the agency.

Neither B&W nor BBDO were very excited about having one of those British filter things to handle. We gave it a nudge in advertising, instead of a push. Two columns in general magazines. A few radio spots. Some car cards.

I wrote the copy, the very first copy for a filter cigarette in America, I believe. There were plenty of different tips—cork, straw and even gold. But none of these were filters.

Would you like to know what my headline and basic theme were? "Don't Pf-f-f-ft Tobacco." Maybe I had better repeat that or you won't believe it. "Don't Pf-f-f-ft Tobacco." Sales responded about as you would expect. The problem of pf-f-f-fting tobacco did not seem to be a very serious one in these parts.

Eventually Viceroy followed Kool up to Bates. They changed its whole character. Made it bare its teeth and fight. My friend Rosser Reeves, I suspect, wrote a wonderful weasel for B&W. In case you haven't heard what a weasel is or was, it is because there have been none around lately. A weasel is an advertising claim that is 100 per cent true. But for the hasty, the glancer or the mentally retarded it is not true at all.

The Bates weasel was "The Tars and Nicotine trapped by the Viceroy Filter can never reach your lungs." True? Of course. Intent? Ah, that's where the trouble comes in. The Federal Trade Commission began to consider intent as well as truth and all the weasels died.

From here on, Viceroy fought the war of the filter traps. They had more than anybody. It was like a poker game. "I'll raise you another 50,000 filter traps." Finally they ran out of numbers and peace ruled once again.

I am, and always will be, a great exponent of truth in advertising. But it *was* more fun when you could lie a little!

Newsletter—September 32, 1938. "We have a visiting Englishman in our midst. He is David Ogilvy and comes to us from Mather and Crowther, London Advertising Agents. He has been in New York since last Spring, studying agency methods. Les Pearl say that Ogilvy is the first Englishman he ever encountered who liked America right off the bat." I liked David then, as I do now, but couldn't bring myself to hire him because we already had an Englishman!

Note from Robley to the recently appointed head of a branch office . . .

When James the Sixth of Scotland became James the First of England he left Edinburgh Castle to go to London.

As he reached the border he had two vagrants brought to him. One he knighted and one he hung, just to prove that he really was the king.

You seem to have knighted a good many people since you were sent out there from New York, but I have not heard of even one hanging!

*Hail to BBD&O*
*They told the nation how to go*
*And managed by advertisement*
*To sell us a new president.*

*Eisenhower hits the spot*
*One full General, that's a lot!*

*Feeling sluggish, feeling sick*
*Take a dose of Ike and Dick.*

*Philip Morris, Lucky Strike*
*Alka Seltzer, I like Ike!*

MARYA MANNES

# 16

☞ Those sly advertising fellows who sell the President as though he were soap or cornflakes have been at it longer than you think.

From the New York *Times* of July 23, 1916, a release from the headquarters of Charles Evans Hughes: The use of an advertising agency would "give the Republican party a permanent organization of trained publicity experts who will now, and for the first time, apply to politics the merchandising principles that are applied to successful business enterprises."

Only newspapers and billboards were available to carry the cause of Mr. Hughes. No one had as yet gotten around to sending words and pictures over the air, and magazines closed too far in advance to handle the quick-changing pace of political strategy.

Students of ancient history will recall that Mr. Hughes gazed out of his suite in the Astor in New York while the votes were still being tallied. Across the street there was a sign "U.S. Tires." "Tomorrow," quipped the candidate, "that sign will read 'U.S. Tires of Wilson.'"

But tomorrow alas the sign was not changed. There was no victory, but a plentitude of alibis.

The twelve states where women could vote went solidly against him. Could it be that women did not like his beard?

William R. Willcox, National Chairman of the Republican Party, felt that the campaign had started too soon. Never before had a Republican presidential candidate started his campaign in midsummer. The heat, noted Mr. Willcox, had its effect. And local attention in the various states was more on their primary fights than upon the national issues. Some felt that Mr. Hughes's reply to a heckler, which was repeated all over, was unfortunate. In answer to the question, "What would you have done when the *Lusitania* was sunk?" Mr. Hughes at great length and circumlocution replied that he would have the nation so strong that the Germans would not have sunk the *Lusitania*.

A New York *Times* staff writer named R. Bean opened up a real mystery. "Not Mr. Hughes," he wrote, "but another must answer for the slump—Mr. A. N. Rodway of Cleveland, Ohio, advance man for William R. Willcox." Rodway had been sent forth on what some western political leaders termed "the most remarkable of adventures." He was first heard of by newspaper men aboard the Hughes campaign train in Utah, although he had been active some time before that. Apparently his main purpose was to reach the next city before Mr. Hughes, discourage any type of demonstration, and see that Mr. Hughes had a closed limousine for his ride to the hotel. There was only a handful of people to meet his train in Salt Lake City, a Republican stronghold. The governor of Utah and the state chairman were humiliated and put the blame on Rodway, who had come preceded by a letter from the national chairman of the GOP.

Rodway, whatever his motive, was pretty successful in making a stuffed shirt out of Hughes until the candidate curtly refused to use closed cars, and directed that orders be given to ignore any further directions from the advance men.

Then there was the famous non-meeting at Long Beach, California, where Senator Hiram Johnson and Mr. Hughes stayed at the same hotel. Each waited for the other to make the first move, and the two did not meet.

But some blame may be put upon the George Batten Company, and the National Committee.

The appropriation—$400,000—was hard to stretch in the face of "Political Rates." This phrase means that Democratic newspapers charged Republicans far more than regular rates—and Republican newspapers did the same to Democrats, naturally.

The Republican planning was sound, as far as it went. We would waste no advertising dollars in states that were surely Republican, or surely Democratic. Our battleground would be the pivotal states.

When it came to California, no one seemed to know whether it was Republican, Democratic or Pivotal. (Do they yet?) No one from the George Batten Company had ever been there—it was four days and five nights on the train. In view of the melting budget and the uncertainty of California's politics, no money was spent there at all. California held the answer, mainly because the time difference made them last to report. The answer was: Charles Evans Hughes lost the state and the election by 3,300 votes. It is hard for an advertising man to believe that a modest newspaper campaign in San Francisco and Los Angeles would not have reversed the answer. So the bad old advertising men were defeated the first time they tried.

I was a highly paid (eight dollars a month) newsboy at the time. I watched for the signal fires that would be lighted up on Mount Wilson—one if Hughes, two if Wilson. But my mother chased me to bed before the fires were lighted.

One paper I peddled carried the story of a Greek who was taking his examination for citizenship. When asked, "Who elects the President of the United States?" he answered, "California," and got his papers forthwith.

We crept back into our kennel and stayed there for thirty years, until our president, Ben Duffy, got chummy with Thomas E. Dewey. The election of 1948 was another cliffhanger, and another loss for BBDO. Mr. Dewey took someone's bad advice instead of our good advice and, feeling quite certain of election, began to preach "Unity." Meanwhile his tireless underdog opponent kept ripping him to pieces before crowds that yelled, "Give 'em Hell, Harry!" Harry won.

A candidate today should, and usually does, make his major media TV. Charles Evans Hughes made a hundred speeches. Granting him an average audience of 10,000, he would have talked to a million people. TV could have given him twenty to thirty million in one appearance. No candidate is ever likely to match the rating of a Bob Hope Special, or the Super Bowl. His audience depends upon two things. First, the general interest in the candidate. But, perhaps even more important, the rating of the show that he pre-empts. It seems difficult for Americans facing a TV set to get up off their bottoms and tune in another program. So a candidate who appears where a top-ten show is usually slotted will keep a large part of that show's audience. In both Eisenhower campaigns he got twice the audience that his opponent drew. And Eisenhower was not the better speaker.

I believe that Eisenhower would have been elected without the help of BBDO or anyone else. But we learned a lot, enjoyed it a lot and may have even helped a bit.

The general's first telecast in the 1952 campaign was from Abilene, Kansas, his birthplace. None of us dared tell the general that he would have to be "made up" for TV. Eisenhower was a rough, tough army man with a real gift for profanity and not the kindly "father image" we remember so well. So we went on a national hookup, with no make-up, outdoors and in the rain. The general came across like the ghost of Hamlet's father after a hard night on the ramparts. There was no question that he must be made up for his next appearance, which was Philadelphia. We sent people to search the beauty parlors of Philadelphia for a real he-man—if possible one who had fought in the war.

Came the night of the speech. The general, already apprised of what must be done, plopped himself into the chair, gave the make-up man an untranslatable stare and gritted his teeth as they tied a bib on him.

"Ever been in the Army, kid?" the general grumped.

"Yes, sir. I was in your old outfit, sir."

"You mean the 101st Airborne?"

"Yes, sir. Purple Heart!"

"Well, I'll be doggoned!"

Make-up was no problem after that and whenever the general

was getting ready for a TV program, he would start the proceedings with his "Paratrooper Story."

We failed, here and there, and one of our outstanding failures was to try to get a local sheriff to memorize: "Ladies and Gentlemen, the next President of the United States."

In Pittsburgh, where the crowd was so great that the auditorium doors had to be barred for safety a full hour before the program was supposed to start, BBDO boosted Fred Waring's entire band through the men's room window.

In Kansas City, we decided to make our own TelePrompTer, for there weren't many around at that time and apparently none in Kansas City. We lettered the general's entire speech on a roll of butcher paper in letters six inches high. We were going to unroll it off-camera as he read. One look at our invention and the general decided to speak extemporaneously.

The major purpose of a political campaign, of course, is to elect your candidate. But as the days go by, and you are always getting the auditorium set up, or riding on a train, a major objective is to get a clean shirt. Eisenhower preferred planes. But much of his time was spent on regular old campaign trains, which always got in town after the stores were closed and left before they opened. At least one group of reporters and agency men hired an automobile and raced the train seventy miles to the next town, reaching the town in time to buy shirts and climb aboard again. They were roundly cheered.

Whether there was any connection between the lack of clean shirts and the fact that 150 fillings fell out of teeth during a four-day trip through the West has never been determined.

One morning only one reporter was awake when the train stopped at a remote prairie station for water, ice and inspection. The general was also awake and when he heard calls of "Hey, Ike," he put on his bathrobe and went out to chat with twenty or thirty section hands, gathered around the rear of the train. Someone asked, "Where's Mamie?" and she also appeared in her bathrobe. The one lucky reporter released the story, and within an hour every photographer and reporter aboard the train was in trouble.

"Where were you?" their editors wired. "Where are the pictures?"

They explained their plight to the general, who said, "Okay, bring your stuff back at the next stop." Both he and Mrs. Eisenhower posed again in their bathrobes, and more than one reporter thought they were very nice people.

The general's sixty-second birthday was on October 14 and his staff presented him with the following poem. Please keep in mind the fact that BBDO had *nothing* to do with its writing.

> *May we slow the pace*
> *Of what is rightly called this race*
> *Just long enough for us to place*
> *On you the marks of our embrace*
> *And drink a toast?*
>
> *To us it is a pleasant chance*
> *To pause in this Crusade's advance*
> *Unhalter shield and holster lance*
> *And greet the happy circumstance*
> *That you were born.*
>
> *We'll banish fret, call off the fray*
> *And take this time to let us say*
> *In feeble words, but heartfelt way*
> *How sad we'd be if on this day*
> *You hadn't been.*
>
> *How sad for all of us who go*
> *With hope more sure and step less slow*
> *Because of you, and doubly so*
> *For all of us who've come to know*
> *And Love you.*
>
> *And when the last motorcade is done*
> *Last speech said, last greeter gone*
> *Last whistle whistled, last flight flown*
> *Win or lose we want it known*
> *We'll always love you.*

The general, who had lived through a lot of things, lived through that.

But the birthday cakes were something else. They came aboard at every stop—big cakes and little cakes, white cakes and yellow cakes, angel cakes and devil's food cakes—some iced crisply, some dripping with goo. The cakes were stacked up on the overhead racks until something could be done with them when the train reached Dallas. But the cakes were unwilling to wait. An air hose broke, the brakes grabbed and the cakes took off like projectiles. There were Congressmen smeared with cakes, and cakes smeared with Congressmen. One Senator in a natty blue suit was found *between cakes,* lying on one cake with another draped across his shoulder.

While the cakey train rolled on, two BBDOers who were supposed to be flying from New Orleans missed their plane.

The ticket agent was having a lot of trouble trying to understand why two Republican workers had to get to San Antonio when a large stranger with the right kind of hat, and the right kind of drawl, said, "You boys go into the bar and get yourselves a drink, while I see what I can do." He was back in half an hour.

"Well, I got him," said the stranger.

"Got who?"

"My pilot, of course. Come on."

He took them to the runway, where a De Havilland Dove was revving up its motors and off they flew in lone grandeur.

Next morning, when they were looking over the platform and equipment being readied in front of the Alamo, a tall Texan asked, "How much would it cost to light her up?" The boys explained that the local committee had already arranged for the lights.

"I don't mean just the platform," explained the Texan. "I mean the whole thing. How much would it cost to light up the whole Alamo?"

"Gee. Who knows. Maybe forty-five hundred!"

"Well, do the best you can, boys!" The stranger peeled four one-thousand-dollar bills and one five-hundred-dollar bill from a roll that seemed undepleted by the subtraction. The boys did their best. The Alamo was well lit.

Motorcades were particularly wearing upon the general. A practiced politician would have stood in the car, bowing right and left, and thinking about what he was going to have for dinner. But when someone yelled, "Hey, Ike!" the general thought he ought to spot the man and wave a personal greeting. The motorcades grew longer, hotter, and slower in the West, and the general was getting fed up with them.

After a particularly poorly planned motorcade coming into Los

Angeles, he demanded with a heavy blast of army-type adjectives to see the man in charge. The victim was shoved into the lion's cage.

"I am the man in charge, sir."

"I know you are and you ought to be shot! What happened?"

"Well, General, it's all here in detail." He handed the general a mimeographed booklet, with "Phase one," "Phase two," etc.

The general grabbed it, and turned instantly to the last page —then slammed it against the wall.

"Thirty-eight pages! The whole goddam invasion of Normandy took less than that!"

During the 1956 campaign, we ran a survey to find out where people got their information about the candidate. Those who were extremely interested in the campaign got information from every source they could find—magazines, newspapers, radio and TV. Those who were lukewarm got their information from newspapers and TV. And those who had no interest at all, got everything they knew from TV. But they *did* get the information, and their vote counted just as much as the vote of a man who really cared.

After two Eisenhower victories (which were also Nixon victories), it seemed only natural that BBDO would be appointed as the agency for Richard Nixon. We would take away the "Madison Avenue Curse" by setting up an entirely new agency, just for the campaign, and draft the best Republicans from all agencies who were willing to lend us a hand. They went on the payroll of "Campaign Associates," which was headed by Carroll Newton, one of BBDO's directors. Since the new temporary agency was set up in the Roosevelt, it was geographically still on Madison Avenue, but psychologically far away.

It had another advantage. It ended the intolerable situation where a Democrat was forced to further the cause of Republicans. As Robley Feland put it away back in the Hughes days: "The spectacle of me, active on behalf of the Republican Party, must make the very hills of Anderson County vomit their scorn!"

I was vacationing in Florida when Newton phoned to say that the Vice-President wanted to see us. He was in the hospital with a knee injury.

"Why do you suppose Kennedy wants to debate me?" Mr. Nixon asked. Carroll, who was always a trifle short on tact, said,

"That's easy, sir. Women are going to decide this election and Kennedy is good-looking. You're not." Mr. Nixon said he had no intention of debating anyone, but was just curious. He turned to me.

"What do *you* think is wrong with my campaign?"

For the first time in my life I used one of those phrases that advertising men are supposed to converse in daily.

"If you'll pardon the expression, nothing you throw seems to stick to the wall. You need a central basic idea that will be part of every speech. Like Cato. Every time he stood up he said once more, 'Carthage must be destroyed.' And Carthage was destroyed."

The Vice-President seemed interested.

"I suppose you have such an idea."

I did.

"Kennedy is hitting you over the head with what he calls the 'Missile Gap.' I think an even more dangerous gap is the 'Kennedy Gap.' You have been Vice-President for eight years. You have been a member of the National Security Council. It would take a lot of time, maybe a couple of years, for Kennedy to catch up with what you already know about defense. That is the 'Kennedy Gap.' Don't attack him personally. It's not his fault that he is so far behind you. But the 'Kennedy Gap' is a dangerous and risky thing in these days."

Mr. Nixon seemed to like the idea. We showed him some outdoor boards with his picture and the theme. "He understands what peace demands." He felt that the vice-presidential candidate, Henry Cabot Lodge, should be included. Since it was something less than literate to say, "They understands," the idea was dropped. "The Kennedy Gap" was never used either; I believe it would have elected him.

Skipping the Goldwater "Campaign," we find Richard Nixon in 1968 once more a candidate. At his request, relayed through Don Kendall, President of Pepsico, I went to see him in his New York apartment.

Was I interested in working with him again?

I pointed out that if he were elected it would be because people who were in their teens when he last ran voted for him.

"What you need to do is to staff up with all the young people you can find. The last thing you need around is an old guy like me."

He took my suggestion about not having me around without noticeable resistance. He must have taken my advice about surrounding himself with young people, too. With few exceptions they looked quite young on television. One was only thirty.

A Richard Hudnut advertisement to be published in *Harper's Bazaar* caused a small exercise of caution on the magazine's part. "Undoubtedly you have received permission from the proper person for the use of the portrait in the proposed advertisement. May we have a copy of same, please?" But Madame du Barry had been dead at that time 142 years and we found no way to reach her.

---

An American friend of Rudyard Kipling's sent him all the current magazines. To save postage, he tore out the advertisements. This made Rudyard unhappy.

"Tear out all the other stuff," he wrote. "I can do all that myself. But I find the advertisements fascinating."

---

Bruce Barton, who constantly warred against long copy, suggested that our copywriters be supplied with half sheets. He also offered a prize for the best ad killed by a client because it was too interesting and too unusual.

# Big Ben

## 17

☞ Our fearless leader during the Eisenhower campaigns was Ben Duffy—president from 1946 to 1956. He might have been our president much longer had he not suffered a crippling stroke.

It was very difficult to see Ben because his office was usually filled with people who had just dropped in to say "hello." This was because he was a people lover, and to him all people really were created equal. His circle of friends was large enough to include Dwight Eisenhower and some boyhood pals who were occasionally on the lam.

Duffy would never have said, as Bruce Barton once said when asked what to do about Juvenile Delinquency: "Every time you catch one of the little bastards, sew him in a sack, and drop him into the Hudson." I would have said that, had I been bright enough, but not Ben.

Because it was a people problem, he would have thought seriously and long about it. Ben loved people the way I love books. The only people he didn't love were those who let him down, or botched a job, or made a boo-boo. Even then, he seldom fired such a man. He just ignored him. Looking back, I cannot recall that he *ever* fired anyone, although he sometimes had them transferred to a department where he couldn't see them. Anyway, there were plenty around that needed firing, and got it eventually.

Ben's trouble, and it troubled him all his life, was that he was a souped-up engine in a frail chassis. His physical assembly could not keep up with his desire to excel, or with the brain that sat in the driver's seat. Like all the other kids who lived on West Thirty-fifth Street, he jumped ice wagons, swam naked in the North River, dodged the cops and enjoyed the political carnivals of the local Tammany powers. But even then, he was a frail kid. He told me once that the other kids called him "little slack ass."

The family doctor came up with the answer: beer. Every morning at eleven, the teacher at St. Michael's would announce: "Time for your beer, Bernard." Duffy would trot all the way home, drink a bottle of beer his mother had waiting for him, and trot back to school.

Years later, Ben Fairless of United States Steel complained of the dismal view out of his window. Part of the view was Hell's Kitchen. Ben Duffy pointed out one particular tenement. "I grew up in that one," he said, and suggested that Mr. Fairless go over there and visit it to see what fine people lived there. He loved West Thirty-fifth Street still.

The Duffys gave their meat trade to an Irish butcher in the same block. There was a formula for getting a little extra hamburger. The butcher and his customers understood it perfectly. Ben, who was just a bit taller than the butcher's block, would reach up with a quarter in his hand and say, "Gimme twenty-five cents worth of hamburger and me mither had a very big wash today." The butcher would add an extra patty to the 25¢ worth.

But the friendly Irishman sold out to a German, and Duffy failed to note the change in management. Reaching up, sort of Oliver Twisty, he repeated the magic formula about "mither's hard wash." The German leaned over the counter and over the small Duffy and asked, "Und, lettle poy, who geeves a sheet?"

Ben was just not meant to be robust. Harkness Pavilion became his club. I sat with him all night on the train from Akron. His ulcer was bleeding. By the time we reached New York and an ambulance crew lifted him through the window, it was hard to tell where the sheet left off and Ben began.

I came back from Europe to find that he was again in the hospital, "Just for a checkup."

"Hi, Charlie," he said. "How do you spell occlusion?"

All together, he told me, he figured that he had been in Harkness twenty-five times. One time, he claimed, he had changed his pajamas for street clothes with a visiting client, and gone out on the town for the evening. But we must remember that he was Irish. His parents, in fact, came from very near Blarney Castle.

Ben was a dropout from Regis High School, seventeen years old and working as an errand boy for the Arbuckle Coffee Company. His brother John was working for a very new agency named BDO. Bruce Barton asked John: "Are there any more at home like you?" Ben became the twelfth employee of BDO.

Two things attracted Ben to BDO, a salary increase of $1.75 a week and a desire to be an artist. Nothing kept him from becoming an artist except a certain inability to draw anything but a doodle of a trap drummer with all of his traps and drums. He called this creation "Cornelius." Whether this had anything to do with the fact that Ben's middle name was Cornelius I will leave to some psychiatrist, or other Sin-Diver.

Ben spent two or three days locating Bruce Barton's office. Then one day after Bruce's five o'clock whistle had blown he walked in and sat in the Presidential Chair. Legend has it that Bruce returned and found him there, but it is enough to say that other kids found him there, and dubbed him "Mr. Three-Minute President." The seat apparently felt all right, although it took almost a quarter of a century to convince everyone else that he belonged there.

Seven years after joining BDO, at the age of twenty-four, he was head of the media department, the purchasing department for space. Indeed he was already well known enough to get outside offers. A man from an agency "that does not fool around" told Ben that he knew exactly what Ben was making—$9,000— and he was prepared to offer more. Ben, who was making $2,800, turned the offer down. Senator Capper, publisher of *Capper's*

*Weekly,* had an idea that gave Ben an idea. Said Senator Capper: "The automobile manufacturers will never get roads in the farm areas, unless they first sell the people on buying automobiles. All of them are perfectly happy unless you advertise to them, and the more you advertise the more they will begin to buy new cars, and thereby they will want new roads."

Ben saw an advertising campaign in this to run in small-town papers, "papers twice removed from the big cities." He showed Bruce the rough idea, and Bruce immediately phoned his friend Alfred P. Sloan, head of General Motors.

Mr. Sloan liked the idea. "Bring it over tomorrow," he said, probably never stopping to think that a whole campaign cannot be put together overnight. But it was.

General Motors bought the idea of a company campaign to run in 2,000 small-town papers. The $800,000 budget was a large one then. Hearing the news, Roy Durstine was so elated that he doubled Ben's salary. Ben's boss in the management of BDO was a bit grumpy about a man's salary being doubled without him being in on it.

"I hope you realize," he told Ben, "that this is the last raise you will ever get in BDO."

Ben was a devout Catholic and a Knight of Malta, the highest order a layman can attain. But religion never blotted out superstition in Ben. He had a "new business tie" that he wore to every presentation but one. On that occasion it worked better even though absent than it occasionally did when present.

Ben was basking in Lauderdale. (Lately the story locale has been changed to Palm Beach, I know not why.) He got a call from his assistant, Jim McGarry. The Lucky Strike account was coming unstuck from its present agency. The call to McGarry was from John Coleman, the recognized authority on tobacco stocks, and a buddy from the ice-wagon-jumping days. Duffy dictated a note over the phone to his secretary. It was to go to Vincent Riggio, President of American Tobacco, asking for an appointment next morning. Then he flew back and phoned next morning to confirm the day and hour. The answer from Mr. Riggio's secretary was, "Come over now." Ben had no charts, no anything except some notes he had made on the plane. He came out with the ten-million-dollar account. One of his big problems, he reported later, was what brand of cigarettes to smoke.

Luckies would be too obvious. Anything else would certainly be abrasive. So he took no cigarettes at all . . . patted his pockets anxiously . . . and accepted Mr. Riggio's offer of Luckies.

One man getting an account that size from a stranger was so unusual that rumors started. It was said that John Coleman, the expert on tobacco stocks, and Vic Zaminski, who was then president of Union News, perhaps the largest customer of American Tobacco, had eased the way for Ben a bit before calling him.

But the fact remains that Duffy got the account and the details matter little. At a single stroke Ben had taken us into the big league of advertising. No more were we "Barton's institutional agency" but "Duffy's package goods outfit."

Only one man was unhappy . . . Robley Feland.

"Did any of you ever read Steinbeck's 'The Pearl'?" he asked. Naturally not, but we soon hunted it up. It is a tale of a South Sea Paradise Island, where the natives were happy and content, diving for pearls. One day a diver brought up a huge pearl worth many thousands of dollars. The great pearl brought with it sins formerly unknown on the island—thievery, lying and murder.

What Robley really resented was progress. Powerful strangers would invade our cozy little club of underpaid peons. They might attract other powerful strangers and the place would never be the same. And that is exactly what happened, thank God.

We put in cigarette machines, every column stacked with Lucky Strike. It was called the Russian Voting Machine.

Since Vic Zaminski was president of Union News and Union News operated the Rainbow Room, we had one of the damnedest parties you ever saw. There must have been sixty of us, gathered around a great circular table. The letters LS/MFT wrought in solid ice were large enough to kill a man if they fell on him. There was an accordionist who, among other things, stood behind Ben and Vincent Riggio playing "Let Me Call You Sweetheart."

A couple of years earlier I had been invited to have lunch with the Executive Committee. This filled me with curiosity, but hardly with delight. The last time they had honored me thus, they had cut my salary. This time things turned out a bit better.

Ben was to be elected president at the next Board meeting, and two of us were to be elected executive vice-presidents, J. Davis Danforth—in charge of client services, and I in charge of creative departments. Jack Cornelius was already Executive V.P.

in Charge of Western Offices. Fred Manchee was elected Executive Vice-President in Charge of Research and Marketing a little later.

Walking back to the office with my old pal Robley Feland, I said, "I suppose this means that I am on the Executive Committee, too."

"Certainly not!" snorted my dear friend.

"Don't you realize that I can get on the Executive Committee if I want to?" I asked. "All I have to do is have someone nominate me at the Board meeting and I will be elected!"

"I have considered that possibility," said Robley, "and I know what to do. If you should get yourself elected to the Executive Committee, another committee, called the Finance Committee, will be appointed by the president. It will run the affairs of the company. The Executive Committee will continue to exist, but it will never meet."

"Thanks a lot . . . I'll think of something." It was actually five more years before I joined that sacred club.

By 1952, BBDO was mixed up in several Political campaigns . . . Eisenhower for President . . . Dewey for governor . . . then there was John F. Kennedy, who wanted to be a schoolteacher.

Joe Kennedy was a higher-up in the Catholic Church, as was Ben. They were introduced by Morton Downey. Joseph Kennedy phoned Ben one day. "My son is in the House of Representatives, as you know. But he doesn't like it much. I think he could beat Lodge out for the Senate. I wish you'd have a talk with him."

"But I'm a Republican!" said Ben. "How should I be helping Democrats?"

"You are also a friend. When will you see him?"

Ben named Washington's Birthday, when the office would be closed. John Kennedy appeared as scheduled. Ben talked with him awhile, then sent him upstairs to talk with Jock Elliot (now chairman of Ogilvy and Mather), who was putting full time on the Dewey campaign. Jock does not remember what was discussed—but what John F. Kennedy did about it seems to be general knowledge.

My secretary, who was against both Eisenhower and Dewey, reported that she had asked her father if her job required her to type out the stuff I was writing for the people she was against.

"You just type whatever Mr. Brower gives you," he advised.

Ben was great at calming raging politicians when necessary.

Dewey blew his top every hour on the hour.

He objected to prompting cards and all the paraphernalia of TV.

"It's a disgrace when the governor of the sovereign state of New York has to be subjected to things like this!"

"I agree with you, Governor." Duffy put a comforting arm over the governor's shoulder. "But, as Jimmy Durante says: 'Dem is the conditions which prevail.'"

Dewey announced to his workers and supporters that he had an antenna which told him instantly, when he got off of a train, whether there was corruption in that town or not.

Then his Thursday-night TV appearance was changed to Friday. No one told him. Another tantrum. How could this happen? Why wasn't I told? Whose fault is this? I want to know what went wrong.

An icy silence settled over the group until Ben spoke up.

"We thought your antenna would tell you!"

Dewey was appeased, even amused.

President Duffy and I were not exactly kindred souls, but we got along as well as an extroverted Irishman and an introverted Dutchman could.

I thought him conceited, and he thought me scatterbrained and I'll settle for both being right. He had a right to be conceited, since he had won every honor that could come to an advertising man, except the Hall of Fame, which is open only to those who have passed on. And he became eligible for that on September 1, 1972.

We used to play a lot of gin rummy on trains and planes. He would put CB for me at the top of one column and G.O. at the top of the other. Then, holding up the scorecard, he would say, "I suppose you know what *that* stands for! G.O. for Great One."

I eventually became a little tired at this bit of gamesmanship and about the fifth time it happened, I said, "Sure I know what G.O. stands for—but you spell God-Awful with an A."

We really became pals after I did the Franciscan booklet. I was summoned to his office by McGarry, and found his table fringed by Catholic clerics. They had put together a booklet intended to recruit boys for the priesthood. A Protestant gets a "call," a Catholic finds a "vocation" but there hasn't been much of either any more. One of the best preachers in New York had an anguished time making up his mind whether to become a minister or take over a Ford agency. So these Catholics were recruiting and wanted help from a lukewarm Protestant.

The cover of the booklet showed the head of Christ with the crown of thorns, blood running down his face. The title was "FOLLOW ME!"

Either Franciscans are mind readers, or I am not sufficiently deadpan. One of them said, "You needn't go any further, Charlie. We know what you think. You think it stinks."

"Yes, Father," I admitted reverently, "it stinks!"

"Can you explain why it stinks?"

"It's all manufacturer's bellyache and no consumer benefit."

"Just leave it here," said Ben airily. "Charlie will fix it up for you."

Actually, it wasn't too much of a job.

My title was "How to become a Leader of Men."

My cover illustration was a lad about fifteen. A shaft of light from above illuminated his freckled face. He wore a hat popular at that time—the crown of his old man's fedora, with bottle caps decorating it. The center spread was a checklist, "How to Tell If You Have a Vocation." If you scored above seventy, you were one who should join the priesthood. You would have to be real stupid to score less.

The booklet went through the church authorities without a change. One of the fathers said, "Whether you think so or not, you have to be religious to write such a religious book."

"To be honest, Father," I answered, "it is just as though a group of plumbers wanted me to write a book about plumbing. I'd read up on plumbing, interview plumbers, maybe do a few days' apprenticeship.

"And when I had finished, they would say, 'You must be a good plumber to write such a good book about plumbing!'"

The Franciscans thought it would be nice to celebrate. And we did that, at the Roosevelt Men's Bar. Franciscans are pledged to poverty. A lot of people achieve poverty without trying, but these fellows have to take a pledge. So I got the check, and they promised to pray for me. And they're still at it. I can tell.

Search all your parks
In all your cities
You'll find no statues
Of committees

---

Elderly copy chiefs (forty) never made things easy for a young man. Keith Kimball remembers an experience with his supervisor, Blankenbaker.

Keith was rather proud of the copy he submitted, but not for long.

"How old are you?" Blankenbaker asked.

"Twenty-two, sir."

"Look out the window and tell me what you see."

"Cars, people, sunshine."

"Ah, yes. Sunshine. Do you know what is going on at Yankee Stadium right now?"

"The Yanks are playing the Senators."

"There you have it. You are young. It is spring. And the Yanks are playing. Wouldn't we both be better off if you went to the ball game instead of bothering a tired old man with this kind of crap?"

# Nobody
## remembers
## Mr. Whosis

# 18

☞ If a company is the shadow of a man, then the man must not be a shadow himself. It is no asset in going after new business to be known as "Whosis, the president of BBDO." A writer of advertising gets little publicity and no by-lines. And even the fact that you have been elected is of interest only to your wife, and a small group of agencies scattered around the country—a group small enough to enjoy a football game together without crowding up the Los Angeles Coliseum too much.

The answer for me seemed to be personal appearances, and since I am neither a singer, tap dancer, kazoo player or comedian, giving speeches in places where the press might pick them up seemed to be the answer. The best of these are New York, Washington and Los Angeles or Chicago.

There is never any trouble getting a podium to speak from. All over America there are men called "Luncheon Chairmen" running around with nets like dogcatchers trying to nab a speaker for a convention, a civic club, or The Old Guard.

I had long since gone through an agonizing training in public speaking. I was no Bill Benton when I made my first appearance at those Monday morning meetings. My notes fluttered from shaking fingers, my knees banged together audibly and visibly.

Mostly it made me hopping mad to be such a coward when I was supposed to be tough, so I kept seeking chances to speak at our own conventions, client staff meetings, anything I could find. Only modesty prevents me from telling you that I became rather good and by the time I became president I was really enjoying this talking business.

I seldom, and only under compulsion, spoke about advertising. That gets you into the advertising columns at best. I talked about the fact that tearing down all fences, and destroying all compasses does not make you free. It only gets you lost. I talked about what a wonderful word "Square" once was—and what has happened to it. I crusaded against the "Great American Goof-off." Soon I was in wide demand, and could pick my spots, especially since I asked no honorarium, which means money, dough.

However, it is not all sweet and lovely.

For instance, I accepted a date to speak to the Sales Executives Club of Washington, D.C. Two days later I found that my only chance to take a vacation was on the date that I had agreed to speak. So I phoned the S.E. Club and said I would have to ask out.

But distant rumblings were heard all the next week about what kind of a guy would make a date and then break it? So I accepted again. I would take my vacation in Florida as planned —fly from Miami to Washington, and return the next day, right after my speech.

It was not a pleasant flight north. Thunder. Lightning. And enough rain to soak my suitcase, inside the plane. But I was buoyed up by the feeling that they would surely meet me and take me to a friendly neighborhood refreshment stand. Nobody met me and the natives seeking cabs were not friendly. I finally got squashed into a cab that went on a sight-seeing tour of Washington's running gutters before it got to my hotel. I knew that there would be a note in my box when I checked in telling me to join the boys in the friendly neighborhood refreshment stand.

There was a note. Mimeographed. It directed all speakers to come to the West Room at seven-thirty the following morning for indoctrination. I went out and scouted the hotel. There were plenty of signs around plugging the morrow's program, and my name was even on them. But no people that I knew, or even thought I knew.

I slept fitfully, but was up in time to have breakfast and still make the indoctrination meeting in the West Room. But no one else was. A wandering man told me there would be no meeting. "We settled all that at the cocktail party last night. Too bad you got in too late for it." I had been eagerly seeking people at six.

I picked up a program, and found that I was the last speaker of the morning. The old situation, talking to hungry people who hoped to be on the first tee soon after lunch. It was a good audience, however, with a minimum of sneakouts. A few even came up to shake hands—which made them last in the check-room line, along with me, so it was no small sacrifice.

It was three hours before plane time, so I went into the coffee shop. All at once a man sat down at my table. It was the club secretary, the man who had written such nice letters, the man who was supposed to see that I was taken care of. After praising my speech profusely, he got around to what he really wanted.

He wanted a job with BBDO. He didn't get it.

I ought also to say that sometimes things are arranged perfectly. People have invited me into their homes and have treated me like a guest . . . even a guest of honor. But the odds are pretty much against it.

The Chairman of the Client's Board grabbed me as I walked past his office on the way to an advertising review with the president. "Come in and sit a minute," he said, "there's plenty of time!" Maybe for him. Not for me.

I walked into his office, gently propelled, and suddenly I had the same sinking feeling you get when the doctor says they will have to operate. Sitting there with a happy grin on his face was a man I knew only too well, a member of the staff of the United Funds and Community Chests of America. The reason I knew him was that we had done his advertising free for twenty-five years.

"We want you to be chairman of this year's drive," the Client

Chairman said. "It won't take too much of your time—the staff does most of the work." I was not unfamiliar with what I would have to do. Make a speech to a meeting of publishers in the East and another to TV-radio people in the West—thanking them for the free time and space they had given last year, and asking for more of same. Plus a few talks in the larger cities. I quickly gave twenty-four reasons why I couldn't do it. The chairman listened with obvious interest, dialed someone on the phone and said, "It's okay, Charlie accepts!"

In such a situation an advertising agency man can do one of two things—he can say "okay" with a smile, or he can say "okay" without a smile.

The United Campaign has its own permanent Board, with its own chairman. I was just chairman of the 1964 Drive. My first job was to go to lunch with the permanent committee in New York and get acquainted.

In New York the morning had gone so well that they decided to finish their meeting before lunch. Several committee heads reported, but the one who interested me most was the chairman of the committee in charge of getting chairmen for the annual drives.

"We've got to get started earlier next year," he said. "And not do what we did this year . . . wait until we have to take anything we can get."

Later, when I was introduced as the chairman for the drive, I reminded them that I had already been introduced as the only man they could get.

In San Francisco, I spoke to the ladies of the Greater Bay area. I had not been introduced to the chic little lady on my left, but she looked slightly familiar and I sneaked a look at her place card: NANCY REAGAN. I almost choked on my mashed potatoes.

When the governor of California was known as "Ronnie" he had been the man who introduced one of our TV shows. I would guess he had been on for eight years. At the end of his contract, we dropped him. We felt that he had been on almost forever, maybe people were ready for a new man in his spot.

Mr. Reagan flew East to protest. We had a legal right to drop him, he admitted, but not a moral right. He was too old for the movies. We had used up his best years and he had no place to go, he would be unable to get a job anywhere.

Nevertheless, we dropped him. And here I was, sitting next to his wife, who certainly must be somewhat bitter in spite of the way things turned out.

I introduced myself to her as chairman of the current drive. No mention of BBDO. I looked at my own place card. Thank goodness, no BBDO there either.

But the chairman of the ladies group did not spare me when she introduced me. She BBDOed it all over the place. I gave my speech. It drew ample applause but it could not go on forever. I sat down and waited for the lightning to strike.

"Why didn't you *tell* me you were with BBDO?" Nancy asked. "Why—Ronnie and I ate off you people for almost ten years!"

If California ever needs a successor to Governor Reagan, my candidate is Nancy!

There were just two speakers scheduled for the morning of this rainy November Tuesday in Dallas, Lyndon Johnson and me. All the soft drink bottlers in the world were there—and all the people who sold equipment to the bottlers. About 2,500 in all, I would guess. Mr. Johnson was scheduled to speak first. Although I was a president and he was only a Vice-President, his outfit was larger than mine. But he was having trouble getting in from Austin. The weather was dismal and windy.

Someone leaned over me, seated in the front row with my wife, and whispered, "The Vice-President is still aloft—you may have to go on first."

"Okay—but remember something. I have worked very hard on this speech. If Johnson and his mob arrive while I am speaking, keep them quiet until I get through." He agreed, and I did go on first.

I believe, it is somewhat hard to remember now, that I was exactly halfway through my speech when I felt a tug on my coat-tail.

"The Vice-President has arrived and he insists on talking right now or else he won't speak at all. I guess you'll have to sit down."

Although I am a rather phlegmatic guy, my wife says I did a very creditable job of tearing my hair and calling upon God to witness the injustice of it all.

I presume that Johnson's talk was his standard talk, since he was able to give it while watching his watch. He said that most of us probably did not realize how the per capita debt of the United States had dropped since John Kennedy became President. This annoyed me, because the credit obviously belonged to the bedrooms which had produced the percaps, and not to the Administration. Finally he left to keep his date with "Barefoot Sanders." I do not know "Barefoot" but, since it was his appointment that ruined my speech, I remember it.

What do you do with half a speech? I clambered back to the podium still wondering, when I became conscious of a great noise down front. People were clapping their hands, whistling and every one of them standing up. They were *for* me!

This one time, having a tongue that is faster than my brain was a great asset.

"Don't feel sorry for me, folks," I said. "The way things are these days, even the best programs are interrupted by commercials!"

Then the pandemonium cut loose again.

"Funny thing," a friend told me later. "I was in exactly the same position with Harry Truman. The only difference was that he stayed out of the auditorium when he heard that I was already talking. 'Let the young feller finish,' Truman said. 'I've got plenty of friends out here. I'll just walk around and visit until they're ready for me.'"

Enough of speeches, except I'll tell you how to get even with people who don't like you. Several of my speeches were reprinted in the *Reader's Digest*. I got a particularly nasty note from an agency man, stationed in Atlanta. It was a really vile letter, which I can't repeat in this family publication. The idiot sent it on his company's stationery. So it was no trick at all to write to his boss, repeating what had been said, and suggesting that he surely did not want such a man in his company. Then I tore the letter up and sent the carbon to the offender. Try it sometime. The only trouble is you never get a chance to see the man suffer.

When Bill Zeckendorf was our landlord, luxuriating in a penthouse on our roof at 383 Madison, Monsignor (now Bishop) Sheen asked Pat, the elevator man, for directions to Bill's office.

Pat told him, let the elevator door close gently behind him and whispered, "There goes St. Pat's."

---

Among the malapropisms I have picked up off the floor in my and other offices, and added to my collection are these:

A problem with many faucets.

A secret cow.

A singing commercial with a reprieve at the end.

An account executive who exhumed enthusiasm.

A flaw in the ointment.

A problem viewed calmly in an atmosphere of complete distraction.

# Who could love an advertising agency?

## 19

☞ Once, and briefly, I was a client. There were so many "Assts." between the top guy and me that I was almost not around. Only my paymaster knew. I did think it odd that we were running full pages in *The Saturday Evening Post* with artwork by the expensive John La Gatta, when nobody could identify our yard goods because it was not branded. But I knew, even then, that, should you discover that the man up front is an idiot, he will thank you for helping him keep his secret.

I became an agency man after being worked over by one of my bosses, who even took me to the 1928 meeting of the Association of National Advertisers. For a couple of days he explained, with gestures and reasonably good whiskey, how unstable the agency business was. Unquestionably I would be dropped from the tenth-floor window on my ass the first time an account was lost. I have probably helped get more business and lose more business than any man who, like me, is medically alive. But the only time I ever felt insecure was when I looked back at what went on in my early days. Like those guys tossing a penny to see if I would go or stay. Like getting married in the first year of the depression and having a child the next.

Any agency that doesn't lose business still has wet paint on its shingle. Ogilvy loses business. Wells, Rich loses business, Y&R loses business. Bill Free loses business. J. Walter Thompson loses business. Doyle, Dane loses business. If there is a small boutique somewhere that has never lost an account, keep a low profile. Ted Bates in his first years as an agency president never lost a single account. Then his boys began to talk about it when— "BANG"—one of their little balloons popped right in their faces.

It may sound negative to be talking about losing accounts instead of keeping them. But sometimes the negative is stronger. As Bruce used to say, "Try writing the Ten Commandments positively."

There are only three situations where an agency can lose an account. When sales are bad and a chair must be kicked. When sales are good and the client has time to look around. When sales are just so-so and the client feels that "some fresh thinking is needed."

There is of course the new broom who isn't smart enough to understand that the *old* broom knows where the dirt is. Mergers may bring you a new boss who doesn't like the way you look through his bifocals. And there is the new son-in-law who works for another agency. But these are more rare.

I always feel when I read that wonderfully redundant phrase "mutually disagreed," or even "mutually agreed," that it is bullshit. It is great trouble to a client to have to change agencies. He has to listen to a half dozen agencies make two-hour presentations. Even if his mind is already made up—he still has to listen to half a dozen agencies to make the switch seem thoughtful and legit. And weeding them out is difficult. Clients and agencies seldom come apart over a single thing, but because of a long series of small abrasive errors and misunderstandings—coupled with boredom at seeing the same old people, and getting the same old answers. I maintain that every client loss is the fault of the agency. Even with new brooms, mergers and sons-in-law. None of these situations would result in lost business if the agency had behind it a history of such great campaigns that it seemed dangerous to lose the agency.

The first thing for any agency to remember is that clients are seldom dumb. They have a higher percentage of business school graduates than agencies do. They live in bigger houses, drive newer cars, have healthier bank accounts. For years I have told writers and others, "Don't you drive by the client's palatial estate in your old beat-up jalopy and then tell me he's dumb! Obviously, someone is dumb, and it just might be you."

But the grass is always a little greener on the other side of Madison Avenue. One of our clients was trying to convince us that Doyle, Dane, Bernbach was better creatively than we were. Just a lunchtime needle. We took the negative in this little debate. "Anyway, you'll have to agree that their Air France stuff is just great!" And we did agree, because at that time we were doing the Air France advertising. I have been in more than one situation where client A wanted to know why we couldn't do a campaign for him as good as the one we were doing for client B. At the same time client B was asking why he couldn't get some of that good stuff client A was getting.

We once had a client whose advertising manager was the purchasing agent for the company. He bought advertising along with raw materials, fuel and office furniture. This client had another agency beside us. The client, a real card, told us about a slick trick they had played on this other agency. When noontime came, the agency had almost finished its presentation, and left the layouts tacked up on the wall while they went to lunch. They did not lunch together. The client's people got back early and rifled the agency's package, finding some sketches that made no sense at all to them. They replaced the ads on the wall with these incomprehensible layouts. When the agency returned, the client —those jokers—asked, "Why did you waste the whole morning on that other campaign, when you had this wonderful stuff?" The agency writer, using less than 1 tsp. of sense, whispered loudly to his boss, "I told you this was the one we should have shown first."

The client's people rocked with laughter.

"Take it down," they choked. "It's a lot of shit!"

Strangely enough that same agency works for that same client after all these years. We weren't funny enough to keep our part of the business.

Not many clients want to be all this funny, when they are joking about several million dollars. But most of them secretly believe there is a Holy Grail, and some agency has it—some magic phrase, some electrifying idea that would double sales. But, fellows, there is no magic in advertising. Enough guts, sweat, talent and devotion on the agency's part . . . along with courage, belief and persistence on the client's part, can sometimes make results that look like magic.

Most clients expect, indeed demand, great consumer campaigns. But it's the *little* good things you did, when you really didn't have to, that endear you to them.

I arrived at a client's office one afternoon and found him woefully studying the dummy of a booklet prepared by his PR firm. He was due to present it to his management next morning and it was somewhat less than average in excellence. I told him to get me a typewriter, some paper, and notify the night watchman, and I would have his booklet rewritten in time for the meeting. But, he pointed out, that will take you all night. It did, too. But after that I could do no wrong as far as he was concerned.

Clients sometimes complain that they do not have enough contact with the "principals" of the agency. They could, if they were with a smaller agency, they point out. Strangely, only in connection with advertising do they feel this way. They do not seek out the smallest bank or even the barber who is never busy. They do not patronize the doctor whose waiting room is always empty. They do not take their cars to mechanics who can go to work instantly because they only have one or two other customers.

One way to lose an account is to neglect the little people in a client's office. You will not have to wait until they grow up and fire you. They are with the boss more often than you are. A grain of sand here, a grain of sand there, can build up to dangerous grinding noises.

Clients do not like agencies that take too many bows during a season of success. They figure that they had something to do with it.

Clients do not like contact men who are too stubborn, nor those who give up too easily.

Clients do not like contact men who are too old or too young. They like them *their* age.

Clients do not like contact men who talk too much, or those with nothing to say.

Above all, clients do not like contact men who lie.

I have a friend, named George Theophilopoulos, who has an advertising agency in Athens. He told me that he had fired one of his very best men.

"But why, George?" I asked.

"He did not feel the agony of the business," said George.

Clients like advertising men who "feel the agony of the client's business." Which translated into English means a man who cares so much that it hurts.

Our friends at Young and Rubicam did some promotional work for Sam Goldwyn (circa 1939–40). Being pleased with them, he suggested that they name his new movie. It was a typical boy-girl nothing much. After some head scratching the boys came up with *Escapade*.

Goldwyn turned it down instantly—"Half the people will think it means a jail break."

Another Goldwynism? They lettered the word "Escapade" on pieces of cardboard, and went about the city showing people the sign and asking what the word meant.

Half thought it meant "Jail Break." Mr. Goldwyn named his picture *Her Wonderful Night* and went right on making money.

# There's
# no business
# like
# new business

## 20

☞ To quote a great man who will recognize the quote, "Every advertising agency is like a leaky bucket. You have to keep pouring it in at the top, or one day you will find yourself empty."

In England there is a gentleman's agreement that no advertising agency will solicit another agency's account unless invited to do so by the client. But over here in the Land of the Free a "gentleman's agreement" is collusion, and you could go to jail if they find an empty cell. So new business contacts are made every day by every agency that can get by the door. We lost a bank client in Boston last year and 140 buzzards circled the scene, hoping for an invitation to land.

I have never seen a new business presentation that I was not involved in. I would like to see one before I join that great copy department in the sky. I wonder if other agencies have as much trouble as we do.

The bulb in the projector burns out. Some needed extension cord was forgotten. A couple of case histories we especially wanted to show are not in the package, and we notice for the first time that the lettering man left the *r* out of "shirt." We probably have the only president who carries a spare bulb in his pocket and insists that everyone who appears in a new business solicitation know how to run and/or repair the projector.

From time to time, I have figured that such breakdowns are our substitute for Charisma. Obviously we are not Madison Avenue Slickers. Because we are so unsmooth the prospect feels comfortable with us.

One time the error, if you could call it that, was a lady director (we used to have one before Fem-Lib). Jean Rindlaub was in the middle of her talk, when the prospect, who had shown symptoms of coming our way at lunch, said, "So okay, you have the business. Now let's cut out the speeches." Jean was indignant, although she must have been as happy to get the business as the rest of us.

"I spent three nights and a weekend on this speech," she said, "and I . . . AM . . . GOING . . . TO . . . FINISH . . . IT!" Which she did, with no apparent damage.

One of our officers got a call from a national advertiser saying that two of his men and a consultant would like to stop in tomorrow and ask a few questions. The consultant was Ray Rubicam, retired co-founder of Young and Rubicam. When they came in they asked questions that showed it was no casual meeting but an all-out presentation for which we were totally unprepared. We kept people running back and forth getting proofs and tapes, but altogether it was a sad performance. Ray Rubicam obviously felt that he was wasting his time. Finally he got up, stretched, yawned and said: "It's pretty obvious that there is nothing much here for us. But thank you, gentlemen!"

Suddenly, I was enraged, a rare thing for me. I forgot that Ben Duffy was in charge of the meeting. I was just there as head of creative departments.

"Damn you, Ray." I may have even gritted my teeth. "You haven't even given us a chance! I dare you to come back at eight o'clock tomorrow morning and see a real presentation!"

"Make it nine," said Ray.

We worked all night putting our story together in logical form. We also got the business.

Why don't we have a standard presentation, ready to give at a moment's notice? Because everybody's business is different, and he wants to know what we can do for his business. We can tell him about BBDO, but that is equivalent to showing the factory. Prospects who may be beginning to doze, become suddenly alert when you give them some facts about their business or their industry.

One prospect (we didn't even know he was a prospect until he phoned) asked us to prepare three speculative campaigns for three different problems he faced. They allowed us a month to get ready—and it took three teams most of the month to collect data and make ads and commercials. Time and money spent amounted easily to $50,000. When they appeared in the afternoon, they had had a Board meeting in the morning and fired the president. He came along, too. They held little rump meetings inside our meeting and paid scant attention to any of our presentation. As they walked out I heard one of them say, "I think we'd do better at the XYZ Agency." So to the XYZ Agency they went, for a few months. Then all at once they switched again.

What happened? The new president they brought in was from the West. He knew which town he was going to live in, but very few people in the town. He was introduced to a man who knew the town—and all its people—very well. He even helped the new president choose a house. They became fast friends.

One day the new president asked, "Isn't that agency you work for a pretty good agency?" It turned out that it was (and indeed it is). "Then why aren't you working for me?" The helpful man was willing. Here, Bub, take this $11,000,000 and run along.

Batten's dictum "I go anywhere for business" still holds—but his exceptions are gone. We go to saloons and other questionable rendezvous, go to the golf links, and the theater, and the opera and other places of amusement to inveigle business under the guise of friendship.

We figure it is easier to get business some day in the future from a friend instead of from a stranger. But making friends does not always work out so well.

Bruce was spending a weekend aboard a yacht with the president of the Santa Fe Railroad, a dignified elderly gentleman with a white goatee. They were anchored off Lloyd, or some such harbor. Being elderly, the president woke early, and Bruce joined him up on deck. The fog had not lifted and visibility was low, when out of the fog came a canoe paddled along by two young girls. They circled the cruiser once or twice, obviously interested in seeing a boat that large and luxurious. With the courtesy typical of his time, the president called out, "Would you two young ladies like to come aboard and see the inside of the ship?"

The girls suddenly turned shoreward and paddled double speed. "Go on, you old goat," one called back. "All you want to do is get us aboard and fuck us."

There is no record that we ever got the account.

Benton and Bowles, BBDO's Prodigal Sons, made their tiny agency into a big one with one new account. The only headline I remember before they got big was "For every pound of Adolph Goebel's sausage you buy, we'll give 1¢ toward the repeal of prohibition."

But the boys had a Yale friend whose father was a big man at General Foods. I believe it was Chester Colby. Bill and Chet consulted him on every move they made, even to hiring secretaries, and thus got him both interested and involved in their efforts to build an agency.

Meanwhile, one of the really big agencies, Erwin, Wasey, had, among its accounts, General Foods and Camel Cigarettes. Camel was publicizing a great forward step in cigarette freshness. They were going to wrap every package in cellophane, something no other cigarette had done.

Camel, presumably, was happy about the great campaign Erwin, Wasey was running for them, but Mr. Colby was not. He felt that everybody in the agency was working for Camel and nobody for General Foods.

So General Foods called in Atherton Hobler, the Erwin, Wasey account executive, and said they would like to move part of their business to Benton and Bowles, if he would go along and help keep the boys from making any really big mistakes. He would, they did and overnight the little agency was in the Big Leagues. Bill Benton and Chet Bowles got out of advertising in their forties (I think Bill was only thirty-six). But Atherton Hobler loved advertising. He stayed. In fact the last I heard he was still there, but coming in less frequently.

The Florida Citrus business is a wandering comet in the advertising skies. It sheds agencies with impressive frequency. Then it sends out invitations to other agencies to come to Lakeland and be part of a circus. Put on a song and dance act about what you would do should you be blessed with the account.

When I got my invitation, Benton and Bowles had the account. I got all of their proofs, and all the kinescopes and radio tapes I could find. I thought they were excellent and wrote a very polite letter to the citrus folks saying that I thought they ought to stay right where they were.

There are apparently factions, or enemies, or something down there, for they kept the wires warm trying to find out who "put me up to it." They figured that no man in his right mind would turn down several million dollars' worth of business. I guess that's why I have such a clean mind—I am always out of it.

After you have won a new account, and had the indoctrination meeting, comes the trip through the factory. Your new client is proud of his factory, which he should be. The least the agency can do is to let him show it off. There are several kinds of factories. Some go thump-thump—squee! Some go jingle-jangle. Some go puckety-cuppity. Some just hum. And some have a bit of each. It is highly unlikely that you will get an advertising idea here . . . it is another step removed from the buyer's question, "What will it do for me?"

Nevertheless, the trip is the time for paying attention. It is a time for asking sensible questions if that is possible. It is a time to be serious.

Jokes about the factory, the product or the client should be saved for another day—better still, forgotten.

An agency group (not ours) was making a trip through their new client's margarine factory. The margarine was being extruded under pressure from a tank with a round hole in it. One agency man looked at the rushing margarine and at the machine, scratched his head and said, "When does it fart?"

The rest of the trip was canceled and so was the newly inked contract.

A sense of humor keeps you alive and sane in this advertising world—but it should have a tight leash on it. Only two U.S. Presidents were noted for their sense of humor—Lincoln and Kennedy. They shot them both.

*Reader's Digest* man: I do wish you'd come up and play the Digest Course with me sometime.

BBDO man: What have you got up there—a three-hole course?

---

When Lever headquarters were in Boston, their advertising director was a character named Grafton Perkins. He would leave the room while you were talking to him, saying, "Go right ahead, I'll be back." We had an argument about putting quotation marks around words in headlines. Grafton claimed it lent emphasis to quote a word. I claimed that it marked the word as not quite true. I won that argument, possibly the only one I ever won with him, by asking: "How would you like to read in the paper tomorrow that Grafton Perkins and his 'wife' spent last night at the Copley Plaza?" The use of quotes for emphasis was dropped.

# Clients
## Four

---

# 21

☞ All clients are different, and the same client is different on different days. Some like to play games. Some like to play the Great Dictator. Some are too little for their job. Some are too big. Some obviously enjoy their jobs. Some dislike theirs. Some, indeed, may not even like their agency but fear to change lest they do even worse.

The only exceptions are present clients of my former agency, each of whom is perfect. Since there is no news in perfection, I will tell you about imperfections of long ago. Try to stay awake.

Long after Durstine left us and took with him his ban against liquor accounts, we still remained without a liquor account. Then Ben Duffy heard that "The Chairman" was puzzled because Ben had never tried to get any of his business.

Ben called on "The Chairman," and we were appointed the agency for several Schenley accounts. "The Chairman," Lewis S.

Rosenstiel, was Chairman of everything. He hired presidents when he felt the need.

His offices were then in the Empire State Building, but he had a few special offices in the Chanin Building. There were no secretaries in the Chanin offices, no telephones, just pads of paper and pencils. Men who had in some way displeased The Chairman were sentenced to these offices. They were supposed to think, and await the day when they might be summoned again to grace.

The Chairman invited us to a get-together lunch in his private dining room. We guests had stew. The Chairman had a steak. Listening to this powerful character I knew that I would be quickly ground down to a nubbin unless I did something to prove that I wasn't sc-c-c-c-cared. So I addressed him as "Lew." The Empire State Tower rocked a bit, but I am told it always does this.

Later he called me to his home for a "Creative Meeting." I went but I explained what my office hours were, and how much I needed sleep. He was famous for calling people at any hour of the night, inviting them to come to his house to share his insomnia along with a new idea he just had. I didn't want any of that—and I never knew him to have an idea that could not keep until morning.

He was a triumph of studied messiness, cruising about the room in crushed slippers, wearing a maroon robe with just the right touch of egg on the lapel.

Lew was one of those men who struggle for success long after they already have it . . . still making touchdowns when the stands are empty, the other team long gone and the shadows lengthening toward him.

I presume that—like most of us—he was seeking happiness and was baffled because success did not bring it. Success is a sort of failure. You reach the end of the rainbow, but there's no pot of gold. You get your castle in Spain, but there's no plumbing.

Lew, I knew, had long been wild about roosters. He had sent the president of another agency (The Chairman had agencies like a Rosary has beads) to Europe to buy up all the ceramic roosters, metal roosters or other artwork roosters that he could find. None pleased The Chairman.

His idea was that a real happy crowing rooster, named "Sunny

Morning" might convey the idea of "No Hangover" to the whiskey lovers of America without conveying it to the Federal Trade Commission. Eventually he got around to the subject.

"What do you think of roosters?"

I replied that, having spent considerable time on the farm, I considered myself something of an authority on roosters.

"So what do you think of them?"

"They have lice and fuck hens."

One afternoon he had another great idea. He called his current advertising manager and said, "I want Duffy and Brower down here at 2 P.M. I have an idea I want to give them."

The advertising manager said such a meeting was hardly possible, since Mr. Duffy was in the hospital and Mr. Brower was in Europe. Apparently not too upset by this news, he called the same advertising manager later in the day and said, "Charlie Brower is in the hospital. Find out what hospital and send him flowers."

"You've got it wrong," said the advertising manager. "Mr. Brower is in Europe. It's Mr. Duffy who is in the hospital."

The Chairman remained unconvinced.

"You heard me! Charlie Brower is in the hospital. Find out what hospital and send him flowers. AND STOP FIGHTING ME ALL THE TIME!"

The Chairman lived in Greenwich at Conyers Farm, a rather vast estate which included a lake. On this lake floated possibly the only rowboat with a ship-to-shore phone. On his sixty-fifth birthday, I attended a party there. On the lawn was a "birthday cake" constructed by stacking hundreds of jars in layers. Each jar contained a pledge from one of Lew's customers, naming the amount of liquor he agreed to buy. Most of these happy customers were there.

I lined up to shake hands with the Birthday Boy.

"Congratulations, Lew," I said stupidly. "Now that you are sixty-five, you can get Social Security."

He raised his chin regally.

"For men like me there *is* no security."

The Chairman had a bad habit of starting the year with a budget of seven million dollars, and finally ending the year having spent only four. Since we were staffed up for seven million, we had to cut personnel continually. Even then we lost money.

I explained our business to him one day.

"An agency man works for just two things—fun and money. And we're not having either."

We were nearing the end of our relationship anyway, but "whipped in goodness" lit the final fuse. The Chairman had discovered or borrowed a new method of aging whiskey fast by electricity. He wanted a campaign on it, and he insisted that it use his phrase "whipped in goodness."

"Lew," I said, "I know very little about whiskey, and that was learned from the other side of the bar. But this I do know. Whiskey is made in the deep forest. It is made by elves. They drip it painstakingly, drop by drop, from various forest leaves that only they know about. Then they put it away in tiny kegs to age a dozen summers. Whiskey just isn't the thing for scientists, test tubes and instant aging."

Lew didn't exactly fire me. He was much too busy for such trifles—he sent his number three body servant to kiss me off. One bead in Lew's rosary of agencies was Doyle, Dane, Bernbach. Bill Bernbach, an absolutely terrific adman, who enjoys the reputation of telling his clients what they can and can't do, got the business.

Sometimes a tough man meets a tougher man. The campaign that appeared was "whipped in goodness."

The client-agency relationship has been described as a happy marriage with twelve mothers-in-law.

In the case of the Hoffmans there were three brothers, which tripled the number of mothers-in-law.

In those early informal days of radio, the client was allowed in the control booth. In the Hoffman case, they also tried to help Joseph Pasternak direct the orchestra. I know people who will swear that they have seen one brother giving the signal for "louder," the second for "softer" and the third for "just right" all at the same time.

What the brothers were helping direct was the greatest aggregation of musicians ever put together, although no one knew it at that time.

In the orchestra were Benny Goodman and the Dorsey

brothers plus Oscar Levant at the piano, and Jerry Colonna playing trumpet. Singers included Nelson Eddy (at $150 a week), Veronica Wiggins and Margaret Speaks. Total cost $1,800 per show.

Joseph Pasternak was not only the orchestra leader he was also the chief sufferer. The radio audience loved the show (fan mail was the only rating system then) but the Hoffmans did not love the show. They felt that more instruments were needed.

"But there are no more instruments. We have them all!"

"Then invent some!"

Walking through a hotel lobby one of the brothers heard some music that fascinated him.

He hummed it for Pasternak, but the maestro couldn't make much out of a tune that consisted of the same note repeated over and over.

He walked over to the piano.

"Is this it?"

"No."

"Is *this* it?"

"No."

This went on for half an hour, but finally he hit it.

"That's it! That's it! What is it?"

"Orpheus in the Underworld."

"Orpheus, eh? Well, it's bright. It's sparkling. I want it on my show. It's got a real lime-dry tempo! You understand . . . a real lime-dry tempo!"

The thing that really tore it was the Hoffmans' insistence on more brass . . . more brass . . . still more brass.

Pasternak lost his cool.

"Vat you vant," he said, "are donkey farts! Pasternak vill not give you donkey farts."

But the Hoffmans went right on making money until they sold out to Pabst. They had a philosophy.

"It's a poor skipper that goes against the tide. I always say a good skipper waits and goes *with* the tide! There has been an orange tide but it is receding. A grapefruit tide is coming in. I say, let's *hammer* grapefruit."

Clarence, although he was president, still held his union card from the time he worked on the bench, and attended every meeting of the union. He was a great guy, but he had some sort of heart trouble that made him fall asleep in meetings. But he wasn't *too much* asleep. If the poor guy who was making the presentation should stop in puzzlement, Clarence would be wide awake instantly.

"Go ahead! I've heard every word you said, although I don't think very much of it." When the meeting ended he could only turn down the proposition, because he hadn't really heard it.

At the end of one presentation of completed commercials he jumped to his feet and strode out of the projection room shouting, "You have not only wasted my time, but insulted my intelligence." We could hear his office door slam. We looked toward other officers of the company for guidance but they had only shrugs to offer.

We went back to the advertising manager's office to lick our wounds and try to guess what could be the matter, when Clarence popped his head in and asked, "And what did you think *of that?*"

"I think you are a mean man." It just sort of popped out of me. Several times during the morning he stuck his head into our office again and said, "I am *not* a mean man!"

The clock was close to indicating time for lunch in the company cafeteria. I am an authority on company cafeterias and the best of them hold no threat for "21."

Clarence was sitting alone with his back to the door. I explained to him that I was pretty hungry.

"Do you mind if I eat?"

"Don't be a god-damned fool—sit down here and eat with me."

He was nibbling at a children's-size salad.

"What's the idea of the lettuce leaf?"

"I'm dieting. I weigh a hundred and eighty pounds!"

I looked at him admiringly.

"A hundred and eighty pounds of pure muscle."

"A hundred and eighty pounds of pure shit!"

Now that we were friendly again, I asked him what he found wrong with the commercials.

"Those damned idiotic uniforms on our service men. I've never seen uniforms like that!"

Maybe not, but he had okayed drawings for them several

weeks before, and they would be in use by the time the commercials were aired.

I explained the situation as diplomatically as I could.

"Well, okay then," he said, "go ahead and run them. And I am *not* a mean man!"

"I know you're not, and I apologize for saying it."

Somehow I could never help liking these rascals.

Cam Hawley started with the Armstrong Cork Company just when I started at BBDO. Cam thought he was God, and I'm still not sure he wasn't. If not, he was a gifted braggart who apparently had done everything he bragged of doing, although to do them all he would have had to be around 110 years old.

He told how he had taught the chef of one of New York's better restaurants how to make a certain salad. We decided to call his bluff and took him to the same restaurant.

The chef spotted him and came trotting over. "What a pleasure, Mr. Hawley!" And, turning to the rest of us, "He makes better salad than I do!"

At that time we used paintings instead of color photos in advertising Armstrong room interiors. Cam suggested a certain artist he "used to paint with in Provincetown."

We approached the artist warily. Had he ever heard of a man named Cam Hawley?

"Know him? I sure do. We did some painting together one summer in Provincetown."

We never caught him.

But, like all men who are built like bulls and act like them, he was moody, unpredictable and antagonistic.

We had a writer named Joe Wayer, who only got away from Hawley by dying. Among other things, he did campaigns for Armstrong's Acoustical Ceilings. Cam had turned down campaign after campaign, and Joe was frantic. I decided to work with Joe over the weekend.

"We'll do a dozen campaigns—maybe two dozen. He'll have to buy one of them!"

So we worked all weekend and took the six-something to Lancaster Monday morning.

Cam spotted the big bundle as we came through the door.

"Throw that crap in the corner, and let's do a *good* campaign." Cam pulled up his drawing board and prepared to think.

"You don't know whether they are good or bad until you see them."

"Yes I do. They're bad."

"Maybe there's an idea here that you could make right."

We finally got him to look, and one he even took.

The only way I could cope with Cam was with rather obvious irony, which seemed to leave him baffled and temporarily off balance.

He came bursting into our meeting room for a scheduled review, rubbing his hands with delight.

"Well, I did a lot of slaughtering this weekend!"

"On your farm or in the agency?"

"On my farm, you idiot."

"Tell me," I asked, "do you slaughter cattle like other people or do you just choke them to death with your bare hands?"

He looked at me scornfully.

"Let's quit fooling around and get on with the meeting," he said.

We were trying to buy a TV show from NBC. Sylvester Weaver was president of the network, which should date it for you. Cam wanted everyone to be at ease. He said, "I am very easy to get along with. Ask any BBDO people here!"

"And any son-of-a-bitch who says he isn't is fired," I added.

Cam left Armstrong and wrote a whole string of novels beginning with *Executive Suite*. He had many talents and great ones. The only talent he lacked was the ability to get along with people.

Our account executive spent a weekend at Buttonwood Manor —Cam's farm—and was surprised at the obvious feelings of affection between him and his farmhands.

"How come?" our man asked.

"They are not competitive," Cam answered.

For any who may have missed it, a news release dated January 6, 1925, announced that the Taj Mahal was now lighted by Exide Batteries, then one of our clients.

---

Letter from Si Costa accompanying an ad for flexible tubing, headline, "A worm has no elbows."

Dear Bill: Did you ever try to take a picture of a worm? If you are ever faced with this problem I can give you some good advice. A live worm wriggles too much and a dead worm looks dead.

The official BBDO method is to dip him in alcohol until he doesn't give a damn what happens, but retains enough life to look natural.

*Little by little we subtract*
    *Fable and fancy from the fact*
*Part the illusion from the true*
    *And starve upon the residue*

---

# 22

☞ To a writer of advertising copy, research is an acquired taste. He fears the kind of mind that rejects a headline for a fabric "Light as a Cloud," not because it is a withered cliché, but because laboratory tests of the specific gravity of both showed that the fabric was *not* as light as a cloud—so there!

I hereby turn myself in as a late convert. I was the man who wrote, "If Columbus had used modern advertising research methods, a consumer jury would have decided unanimously that the earth was flat, over-aged mariners would have told of the unattractive monsters that waited at the edge of the world, a depth survey of the crew members would have uncovered the fact that they were only in it for the money, Queen Isabella would have cancelled the appropriation, Columbus would never have left harbor, and you and I would all be Indians."

In regard to copy research, I have done those things I ought not to have done, and left undone those things which I ought to have done, and there is no good in me. Amen.

I never met our first copy research department, because he left shortly after he was jailed in Baltimore, and held there until the judge found out what this knocking on doors and asking women questions was all about. Unless the judge has found the answer, our man is probably still there.

John Caples, world-recognized authority on testing, found back in 1934 that the more a test costs, the more likely it is to be worthwhile. He ranked their value as (a) sales tests to see which campaign or medium actually moved merchandise best, (b) inquiry tests, (c) mail tests and (d) opinion tests. Their cost was in this order, with (a) the most expensive.

John also listed at that time the appeals that seemed to work best:

*Money:* Tell people how they can make more money, how they can save more, how they can get rid of money worries.

*News:* Use news headlines and announcements wherever possible.

*Testimonials:* Authentic testimonials from well-known people help increase sales.

*Sex appeal* (It was around even then): Use attractive women to show other women how they can become popular with the opposite sex.

*Reason why:* Give specific consumer benefits.

*Common experience:* If possible, use experiences that occur often and to many people.

*Proof it's good:* For instance, "Double Your Money Back if you don't agree."

*Self-interest:* Tell the reader what he is going to get out of the product that is going to do him some good.

That list deserves looking over even today, although I suggest going lightly on testimonials. I have written and run authentic

testimonials where the reader remembered the "noted" character, but forgot the product.

The first actual test I was involved in was a test of media. It
was a sales test (most expensive but most dependable). We
wanted to find whether newspapers or radio would sell the most
Silver Dust. We picked three cities of comparable demographics
(although the research boys had not yet gotten to appreciate the
impressiveness of long words that others do not understand).
In town A, we ran only newspaper ads, in town B, only radio.
Town C was the control town, in which we ran nothing at all.

Town C, with no advertising of any kind, won.

Some years later, we found out the probable answer. Another
agency made the same kind of test, using six towns instead of
three. Here, too, the town with no advertising won. The answer
was the salesman who covered the area that included the control
town. He was so hopping mad at having no advertising support,
he set out to show those wise guys back in New York. He con-
centrated all his efforts on the control town, temporarily neglect-
ing the rest of his area. He worked double time, begged for good
display space in stores, even talked the product up to customers,
and consequently he really did show those guys.

The least expensive, and the most unreliable of the tests
listed by Caples was the "opinion test." We used to cry as though
someone were standing on our foot when a client said, "I think
I'll just take these ads home and see what the little woman
thinks." Then we would do the very same thing by management
request—we'd be "asked" to take something home to see what
the little woman thinks, and call it research. I was at that time
a highly subversive citizen around the shop. To see if I could not
get the management to dislike me more, I bribed the editor of
the Newsletter to publish my little poem:

> *Kindly ask your wife tonight*
> *What brand of beads she wears*
> *And get ten friends' suggestions*
> *On a name for pickled pears.*
> *Has your opinion changed this year*
> *On color schemes for picks?*
> *Compare a dozen watches for*
> *The passion of their ticks.*

*Drain your car of all its gas*
*And fill with melted butters*
*A prospect's friend would like to know*
*What sort of sound it utters.*
*Please sow this lawnseed in your rug*
*And see if it will grow.*
*Do you prefer oil heat or gas?*
*Just answer "yes" or "no"*
*What are your thoughts on Birdbrain Bob*
*The Hapless Hour Crooner?*
*Send in your answers yesterday*
*We should have had them sooner!*

Advertising research is at its best when it looks back. It is pretty good at counting heads, but not so good at looking into them. When it tries to look into the future it takes on a slight aroma of tea leaves and crystal balls. Women are the most important purchasers of advertised products. How can you determine what she is going to do when she has no idea herself? Over half the purchases made by women in supermarkets are not on her shopping list, and most likely not in her head, when she entered the store. What she did yesterday is a clue to what she might do tomorrow. But only that.

The "opinion test" has been refined and made valuable. A group of women discuss an advertising campaign or a product under the leadership of a trained psychologist. A see-through mirror lets writers and other interested people watch them, and phones enable the lookers to listen—or to suggest approaches to the psychologist. Everything is taped and studied later. To my mind this is the best of all current "opinion" tests, simply because the women are not being made into experts by being asked their opinion. It is like an over-the-fence discussion. Sometimes writers are slightly shocked that women do not seem to understand them. What does "Avoid Nightly Pin-Ups" mean to you? To a lot of women it meant that they had to fix their hair in the daytime.

Everyone wants sound advertising research. The client wants it because advertising is the only thing he buys on faith and he does not like this "pig in a poke" business. The advertising agency wants it because it is easier to sell on facts than on opinion. Writers today want it. How much easier their jobs would be if they were more sure whom they were talking to! Who is the most likely user? Male or female? Education? Occupation or husband's occupation? Children? How many? Children's ages? Approximate family income?

Is there a small group of heavy users? We know, for instance, that 23 per cent of male adults drink 82 per cent of all the beer. Your market, then, is one man in four, roughly, who drinks almost a case a week. What kind of a man is he? We know—our client knows—and all our beer advertising is a rifle shot at him. Others can have the nice water-skiing pictures and the happiness couples. Our man doesn't go water-skiing—nor does he believe that the beautiful girl in the picture looks like his wife or girl friend.

Here are a few other heavy users.

Sixteen per cent of housewives use 62 per cent of cake mixes. What is the profile of the "heavy user"? If it were known, might not a manufacturer be smart to forget all other women in his advertising, and stick to her? Seventeen per cent of women buy 79 per cent of the instant coffee; 11 per cent of *males* buy 74 per cent of breath fresheners. Eighteen per cent of homes use 67 per cent of canned pork and beans; 11 per cent of women use 57 per cent of the cream rinse. Thirteen per cent of adult males buy 89 per cent of digestion aids; 15 per cent of households use 64 per cent of the table syrup.

Thus a "mighty minority" gives most manufacturers the majority of the business they enjoy. If research could furnish the advertising creative people with "consumer profiles" on the large user, they would jump up and down, bark for joy and lick the research man's hand.

David Belasco said that the art of the theater is to give people what they want just before they know they want it. It reminds me of the advice I got from an agriculture college: "The best way to use fertilizer is to put it on top of the season's last snow." How can you tell which is the last snow? It is also the art of advertising to give people what they want just before they know they want it. The only answer is to be lucky, or to be persistent.

Given a chance, people will resist the new and cling to the

familiar. How is this for clinging—it's a BBDO memo, written two years after Lindbergh.

"March 26, 1929. The Publicity Department advises that the first commercial airplane flight from Europe to America will be made sometime in May and carry light freight. However," the department added, "this has all the ear-marks of a stunt and we are sending out this information so our clients will be advised of it."

We know all about the horseless carriage, Fulton's folly and other scorned firsts, but what about communication? Here are a few answers, available to anyone with a History of the Opera.

*Carmen,* by Bizet. It has been said that this great opera was such a failure at first that Bizet died of humiliation and disappointment.

*Madame Butterfly,* by Puccini. The first performance was a great failure. It was greeted by expressions of violent dislike.

*Symphony Number Three in E Flat Major (Eroica),* by Beethoven. The first performance, conducted by the composer, met with no success. Critics openly disliked it. Its second movement, now considered one of the master's greatest creations, was vigorously condemned.

*Symphony Number Six (Pathétique),* by Tchaikovsky. This is Tchaikovsky's greatest work, probably the best-known symphony in the world. Unhappily it made little impression at first.

*La Traviata,* by Verdi. Its first performance was a great failure.

Wagner, Mozart and many others have been victims of "first-sight fright." But is this, perhaps, a musical foible? What about art?

Edouard Manet: Manet's brilliant painting "Déjeuner sur l'herbe," now in the Louvre, was rejected by the tastemakers of 1863.

Eugène Delacroix: The jealous world of official art snubbed him to the end.

Vincent van Gogh: During his lifetime, the only one who believed in him and helped him was his brother.

Many instances of masterpieces that failed at first can be found on the stage. I will cite just one.

*Our Town,* by Thornton Wilder, now considered one of

America's great plays, was a conspicuous flop in its Boston try-out.

I might add that a client, of somewhat lesser stature than the above, walked into my office one day and saw a layout for a new campaign for another client.

"What's that," he said, "a gag? You having a party or something?"

"It's a new campaign; you'll catch it on the air and in the magazines in a week or two."

"Somebody must be a goddam fool."

Research has made no concerted effort to solve two basic problems: (a) When does an advertising campaign begin to show results, and (b) when is it worn out, when do people tire of it? Bruce Barton once presented a campaign to a client who was so happy with it that he had all thirteen advertisements framed and hung on his wall. In a few months he said, "You'd better be thinking of a new campaign, the public is tiring of this one."

Bruce told his client that it was all a puzzle to him. None of the ads had even run yet.

More good campaigns are dropped too soon than have run too long. For one client we have run the same campaign, with almost infinite variations on the same theme. Each year we ask ourselves if it isn't time to drop it. It's almost ten years now. Then we thought of a very simple way to find out whether people were tiring of the campaign or not: ask them how long they thought the commercial theme had run. The average guess was eighteen months!

And how long must a campaign run before its effect is felt? Obviously the answer is different for each different product. And for each type of advertisement or commercial. But just now, I fear, it is not known for any product or campaign.

That same Bruce Barton, who seems to occupy more and more space in this priceless document, went into the New York showroom of Steinway to buy a piano. Unbelievably, an advertising agency man was there trying to discover whether the current Steinway campaign was bringing in customers.

"When did you first decide to buy a Steinway?" he asked.

"About twenty-five years ago," Bruce answered. "It's taken me all this time to get the money together!"

Charles Pinkham, son of Lydia of Vegetable Compound fame,

told some of us that he believed their campaigns started to work about the time they dropped them.

When Claude Robinson was first selling his "Gallup-Robinson" surveys of readership, I said, "But, Claude, there's nothing here that is not known by everyone already."

"But, Charlie," he replied, "don't you know that the major purpose of advertising research is to dramatize the obvious?"

I didn't, and I don't. I realize that much advertising research is like a lamppost to a drunk—it's sometimes used more for support than for illumination. But I believe its objective should be illumination.

The Chrysler Corporation wanted a name for its earliest compact. It was to stand alone and not be a part of any current line produced by the corporation. The list had been boiled down to six when we met to discuss the names.

The president of the corporation (this was pre-Lynn Townsend) said, "They look all right to me; I'd like to add one—Liberty."

"That's fine," I said, "if I can add one too: Valiant."

Now we had eight names. How could we pick *the* one that was best? Not by asking people directly and putting them consciously in the role of judge. We asked them, but they couldn't possibly guess what we were up to.

Here is a list of eight names, our interviewers said. Can you tell us which you think most suitable for a TV set, for a Mixmaster, for a soft drink, for a compact car, for a toaster, for an electric blanket, for a lawn mower, for a motorboat? These are not the exact products. Those are lost and forgotten. Valiant was named by 60 per cent as a name for a compact car.

After a couple of exciting years Valiant became a Plymouth model. But the real surprise to me was that the president's added starter—Liberty—came out bottom. Liberty was what Patrick Henry was willing to give his life for. Liberty is the foundation on which this nation stands. What happened to it that people even said it sounded "tinny and cheap"? Too much use by the wrong kind of people, perhaps. It makes me think that Congress should start a word bank—where the precious words of our land could lie fallow until they have regained their original strength.

In the case of Valiant, research gave us the answer. But often it gives us only a clue. I believe the advertising research man should get all the clues together, and that someone capable of doing it should add a good measure of experienced judgment. Too often we take one clue for the whole answer.

May I quote for you two useful tips from different advertising authorities.

### Thomas Carlyle:
I dinna trust the collective judgement of individual ignorance.

### Fred Petzel,
#### world's champion hog caller for 1926:
You've got to have appeal as well as power in your voice. You've got to convince the hogs that you've got something for them.

The American Tobacco Company (now a division of American Brands) wanted some unusual way to send Christmas cigarettes to the company's friends and stockholders. They made a box in the shape of a book titled *Fine Tobacco*. But who would be the author? Ellis M. Effty, of course! (That is pronounced "LS/MFT," if you are not too quick at such things.)

Surely no one in all the world would be named Ellis M. Effty. But there was, and he wrote a nice letter of appreciation.

---

When the trading stamp craze was at its height, a California lady won a neighborhood contest, and was awarded a free tank of gasoline. She wanted the stamps that go with the purchase of a tankful of gasoline. It was explained to her that no stamps were due her, since the gasoline was given to her.

"Then," she said, "the thing to do is to charge for the gas. My husband pays that bill anyway, and I want those stamps!"

# God
# and the
# creative
# man

## 23

☞ If you have no Bible at home, every motel has one, and they are often opened because of a rumor that some fellow goes about hiding ten-dollar bills in them. The first five words of the Bible, you will find, are, "In the beginning God created . . ." And if creativity was of such importance to God, it ought to be number one with any right-thinking advertising agency.

God, probably on purpose, had to go it alone. He had no consultants, no committees and took no consensus. Under the circumstances, you could hardly expect a perfect job. The earth is not a perfect sphere and it wobbles through eternity, much as some of the rest of us do. But the world got created, and if God had had enough help we would probably all be on the drawing board still.

When agency heads make talks to their people at the Annual Convention somebody usually says, "We must all be creative."

But he doesn't mean it of course. Who needs creative bookkeepers? Or creative phone girls? Or creative mail deliverers? By creative people, I mean those directly engaged in creating advertising . . . writers, art directors, producers and an occasional account executive.

Creating is usually the work of one man, sometimes with able assistants, and often with a boss. An idea doesn't give a damn who has it, but committees don't have them. Committees weigh, ponder, judge, reject or approve. Then they appoint some subcommittees and go home. A group of men, working together, is not necessarily a committee. No man has ever called Christ and His Twelve Disciples a committee.

And sometimes a committee does not know it is a committee. When Mars approached the Earth many years ago, the citizens of a small western town decided to do something about it. They all climbed to the roofs of their barns and, at the agreed moment, they all shouted, "Hello, Mars." Then they climbed down and congratulated each other. "Man, oh Man!" they said. "If there's anybody up there, they sure heard that!" Meanwhile the real work of probing the universe was being carried on by lone men in distant towers who watched and figured, year after year, generation after generation.

Creativity is the ability to have worthwhile ideas. Ideas alone are a dime a dozen. But the ability to have selling ideas within the restrictions of the market—and good selling ideas at that —is not easy. Writing is not enough. Art is not enough. Production is not enough. The ideas are the thing, and the people who have them seem to be more scarce each year. This is because the advertising industry has failed to keep its hiring and training up with its growth. It seems to me that, if we want to preserve this breed of idea people, we should do at least as much for them as the government does for the whooping crane . . . we should protect them against the national mediocrity and encourage them to do their best. In a very small survey I took, 45 per cent admitted they could do better! A pat on the shoulder will buy you a lot of excellence here!

A few more figures from my small survey. Only 17 per cent were over forty, and only two people were over fifty. By fifty you are either a top officer or an errand boy. There are five males for every female among those who reported. Oddly enough seven people failed to mark which sex they belonged to. Maybe it is as hard for them to tell as it is for us who look at them. College graduates and non-college graduates split about fifty–fifty. This is probably because art directors mostly come from art schools, not colleges. Twice as many do not belong to any church or synagogue as do. Eighty per cent own cars, 20 per cent do not. Eighty-two per cent carry life insurance, and a third of these carry more than $50,000. Twelve per cent think they are paid enough, 0 per cent think they are paid too much and the rest are paid too little, sometimes with underlines and exclamation points. Knowing something of their salaries in past years, they are not really hurting. Forty-six per cent consider their chances of getting ahead to be good, 38 per cent think their chances are only fair and 15 per cent really despair. Half of the creative people think they get along fine with clients, 50 per cent think they are so-so at this talent. Nobody has marked himself poor at client relations.

That figure of five males for every female seems a trifle out of line with Fem-Lib thinking. There is no heavy lifting in this business, and I know of no proof that women are not as creative as men. They even create men. Possibly it is because they do not like the agony that goes along with creativity—the awful feeling of a closing date coming on fast, and not an idea in your little mind.

No longer do creative people come from George Batten's "pulpit or plow." They come from everywhere. One man's writer's father was a subway guard.

As far as I know we have no serious mental cases. We never had any, I am told, until I became head of creative departments. I was accused of attracting nuts. I think this is untrue. It is just that in the old days they did not stand out from the crowd.

I began to hear of a writer who, upon entering a client meeting, would ostentatiously put plugs in his ears to protect himself from hearing whatever went on. Another time he took a paperback from his pocket and read it in the meeting.

The client, poor fellow, tried to get his attention by shouting, "Mr. Blank, what do *you* think of these layouts?" Mr. Blank rose with the dignity of a judge and announced: "BBDO pays me to write, not to have opinions about layouts!" Surprisingly, we still have the clients. But not the man.

Jerry, a writer I had let go, phoned my secretary to tell her that he was going to shoot me when I emerged from the building at lunchtime. She suggested the freight elevators, or lunch at my desk. But I was certain that Jerry did not have the guts to shoot anyone.

I was wrong. He "shot" me with a camera, and went off cackling up the street.

Yet creative people do differ from the run of humanity. They are all trying to pass as extroverts—often overdoing the act. They have restless minds that never let them leave their work at the office, but keep them awake at night, leaving them tired and grumpy next day. They are never free of a foreboding of imminent danger, especially when everything is going "too well." They are certain that their idea well has run dry. They share a conviction that their best ideas wind up in the wastebasket because the contact man did a lousy selling job. There is a saying among the males, "I got the idea while shaving," and I believe it's true. After several days of desperation, the creative man says, "To hell with it," and relaxes (as while shaving), and for the first time the idea has a chance to reach him.

These creative people have a sneaking admiration for account executives who know all the headwaiters at all the best places and sometimes, sometimes take them to lunch.

If we want to preserve the breed, let's take a peek at the animals who prey on them. They are the kind of contact men who do not take them to lunch:

*The ring announcer* opens client meetings by announcing: "In this corner, wearing purple trunks and a desperate expression, is Joe Brown, who wrote this campaign and will now explain it to you." He forgot to tell Joe he was going to do this.

*The four-way cold sweat* tries to help everyone. He peeks over the writer's shoulder and says, "Tsk! Tsk!" He helps the art director draw, and worries double time all the time.

*The interpreter* never tells creative people what the client said. He tells them what the client meant! This is because he understands the client better than the client understands himself. This is a truly great gift, and it is regrettable that he is wrong so often.

*The cruise director.* He tells jokes to get everyone in a good humor and it's always the same joke he told last time. He doesn't want things to get too serious. He is sure everything will turn out all right, and sometimes it does.

*Good old Bill* sits on the client's lap. He has held the account for many years. His last constructive thought was in 1956. The client would never ask to have good old Bill taken off the account. But he may have to fire the whole agency to get rid of him.

*The sly fox* wants a campaign ready to take to his client a week from Thursday. Actually he has a date *two* weeks from Thursday. Thus he gains a week in which he may take the campaign back to his den and chew on it. He never gets caught. If he is seen around the office on the day he had said he was to have the client meeting, he says, "Sorry! The client postponed it."

The man who keeps creative people from biting their nails all the way up to their armpits is the *Old Pro*. In the midst of any crisis, he exudes confidence. You feel it and know that it is not phony. He works closely with creative people—not to lead or guide them but just because he likes them. He never takes credit, he gives it away, but somehow it always seems to come bounding back. When a job is exceptionally well done, he sends small notes of thanks, with carbons to management.

Don't expect creative people to be easy to get along with. It seems unlikely that Socrates, Beethoven, Galileo or Michelangelo could have gotten themselves elected to the local Rotary Club.

---

I know not what Babylonian or Egyptian may have chiseled out the first advertisement, but I have always enjoyed this handbill, circulated in London in the seventeenth century:

A favorable opportunity is now offered any person of either sex who would wish to be buried in a gentile manner, by paying one shilling entrance and two pence per week for the benefit of the stock.

The deceased will be furnished as follows: a strong elm coffin covered with superfine black, and finished with two rows around close drove best black Japan nails and adorned by ornamental drops; a handsome plate of inscription, angels above and flowers beneath, and four pairs of handsome handles with strong grips. The coffin is to be well-pitched, lined and ruffled with fine crepe, handsome shroud, cap and pillow.

# "I am sure
# of just
# one thing
# about radio . . .

---

## 24

*When the announcer says, "we have*
*with us in the studio tonight*
*a little lady with a marvelous*
*soprano voice and a little later*
*on we are going to try to persuade*
*her to sing for us"—the odds are*
*1000 to 1 that the little lady*
*will yield to persuasion.*

*—Robley, 1930*

☞ It was almost a neat thirty years between the day in August 1922 when WEAF (now WNBC) broadcast America's first sponsored radio program and the famous evening in October 1952 when Mr. Frank Walsh, electrician and industrial night guard of West Hempstead, L.I., shot his TV set dead because he couldn't stand it anymore. In the twenty-one years since, there is no record of similar shootings. This is because, while the air was getting conditioned beyond all recognition, people also became conditioned. They are able to look without seeing, and to listen without hearing. This is the advertising creative man's greatest problem. How to *make* them see. How to *make* them hear, without sacrificing the selling message.

It all started in a rather small way.

The first commercially sponsored radio program was a ten-minute talk, broadcast over WEAF for the Queensborough Corporation to describe the delights of apartment living in Jackson Heights. One glance at Jackson Heights today and you must agree, it was a very powerful commercial. But no recording was made. It is lost forever. Too bad?

It wasn't the first radio program, just the first sponsored one. Two years before, in September 1920, the Pittsburgh *Sun* carried an ad for Hearns Department Store. It announced that Dr. Frank Conrad, a Westinghouse executive, was broadcasting recorded music experimentally. By purchasing from Hearns a locally hand-made receiving set, you could join the select group that listened to Dr. Conrad's phonograph instead of their own.

Pittsburgh's KDKA must have been a pretty powerful station because a radio nut friend of mine brought the music in pretty well. Good enough to dance to, if you and your partner didn't mind wearing headsets, and being tethered by the wire that led from you to the set. In November of that year Dr. Conrad broadcast the result of Harding's "Front Porch" campaign.

In October of 1923 WEAF got itself hooked up with WJAR, thus forming a two-station network. But the first real network came three years later, when RCA bought WEAF from the American Telephone and Telegraph Company for one million dollars.

A list of such "firsts" could, and probably does, fill a long dull book. But none could tell you about the first broadcast sound of an airplane engine. It was made by gluing pieces of a man's leather belt to the blades of a fan, and rotating the fan against a tom-tom. The belt was contributed by Arthur Pryor, Jr., later the suspender-wearing head of our radio and television department.

A whole race of sound men sprang up. Coconut shells galloped in a box of damp sand as a distant voice cried, "Hi-Yo, Silver . . . awa-a-a-a-a-y." A ball of cellophane rolled about in the hands made a reasonably good crackling fire. One of the hard nuts was how to simulate water being poured into a glass. After much trying someone suggested pouring water into a glass. It worked out just fine.

The advertising agencies, steeped in decades of printer's ink, hardly knew whether radio was a threat or an opportunity. Psychologists assured them that it was neither. People, they pointed out, were 80 per cent eye-minded and only 20 per cent ear-minded. Thus radio could hardly appeal to more than 20 per cent of the population at best. Later, when movie theaters had to reschedule their pictures because no one would come if they had to miss "Amos and Andy," we sought further counsel from the psychologists. But they were all listening to radios and had no time for foolish questions.

The New York *Times* of September 13, 1926, carried an ad announcing The National Broadcasting Company, a subsidiary of RCA. As the world's largest distributor of radio sets, including the entire output of General Electric and Westinghouse, RCA was dissatisfied with the U.S. ownership of only five million sets. It hoped that better programs might get sets into the twenty-six million remaining homes. It was obvious that a number of stations, joined into a network, could afford better talent and better shows than a squabbling mess of independents. Therefore they asked other stations to join them. No monopoly was intended. Makers of competitive sets were free to use the network at regular prices.

"The day has gone," said the advertisement, "when the radio receiving set was a plaything. Now it must be an instrument of service."

To celebrate, NBC broadcast a show over twenty-five stations, offering the improbable combination of Walter Damrosch, Weber and Fields, and Will Rogers.

One of the first competitive set-makers to take advantage of NBC's generous offer was A. Atwater Kent, who manufactured sets under a licensing agreement. Thus he was a competitor, a sponsor and a licensee all at the same time.

As a competitor and a sponsor he was great. But as a licensee he was imperfect. He didn't pay a cent for six years. By the end of such a period NBC became a bit restive.

General Sarnoff phoned Mr. Kent, who begged him not to worry, the money had been put aside. The only question was the amount. Mr. Kent wrote a check for ten million dollars, put it in his pocket and went to see General Sarnoff.

"How much do you figure I owe you?" asked Mr. Kent.

"Not a cent less than ten million dollars."

Mr. Kent handed him the check and, according to my best information, they "had a good laugh." But why, I do not know.

Mr. Kent was also a close friend of President Coolidge's, and in those days before the presentation of deep freezers and vicuña coats was looked at askance, he gave the President twelve radio sets.

When Mr. Hoover followed Cal (who did not choose to run) into the White House the sets were gone. It makes a pretty picture. "Cautious Cal back in the snows of Northampton, listening to twelve sets."

The Atwater Kent Hour, scheduled from 9:15 to 10:15 Sunday nights, featured stars of the Metropolitan Opera Company. It's hard to believe, but the road was full of rocks. The Metropolitan feared that people would no longer come to the opera house when they could stay home and hear the opera free. Everyone was afraid that broadcasting on Sunday night might bring down upon them the wrath of the righteous. The stars feared that the new gadget might not reproduce their voices perfectly. And wasn't singing into a microphone just the least bit undignified anyway?

Dignity came close to being lost one night when the star soprano showed up ten minutes before air time, riotously and belligerently drunk. While the indignant diva was being shoved into a cab, the "taken suddenly ill" announcement was written, and new music ordered up from the station's library. The program was literally put together as it went on the air. The show was over, and everyone was in a state of collapse, when a wire came in from Mr. A. Atwater Kent ordering that his sympathy and two dozen roses be given the little lady at once. This was the only slip-up in the whole show—the "little lady" never got the roses.

There has long been a story going about that a client refused to buy a Sunday afternoon show because "That's when everyone is playing polo." It was true, and we were there.

We did not put the first singing commercial on the air, and we do not know who did. We would guess Pepsi and "Twice as much for a nickel, too." (Remember the nickel?)

We didn't call them singing commercials then, anyway. We called them "theme songs." The Armstrong Quaker Girl all but installed a Quaker Felt-Base Rug in verse.

> *Oh, pardon us if we, suggest there ought to be*
> *An Armstrong Quaker Rug in every home*
> *For always there's a sun room*

> *And often more than one room*
> *That Quaker Rugs will brighten up*
> *Lighten up the housework*
> *A dampened cloth will clean them off*
> *With ease, and furthermore*
> *Beautiful Patterns, low in cost*
> *Are found in every store*
> *So-o-o-o-o-o-o-o-o-o*
> *Pardon us if we suggest there ought to be*
> *An Armstrong Quaker Rug in every home—sweet—home*
> *An Armstrong Quaker Rug in every home!*

And, if that is not enough to send you right down to the store, here is one intended to keep you *out* of the store.

> *Good evening, you have heard of me before (Knock! Knock!)*
> *It's the Fuller man that's knocking at your door*
> *With brushes that are large and small*
> *For kitchen, bathroom, floors and wall*
> *Their famous bristles best of all*
> *But now we'll have some music and some song*
> *And someday when you see me come along*
> *Just tell me how you like the show*
> *That's sent to you by radio*
> *To please you from your friendly Fuller man!*

One of the best known of all singing commercials was Chiquita Banana—voted by navy students in a midwestern university as "the girl they would most like to get into a refrigerator with."

Chiquita has left our bed and board now, but it's hard to forget an old sweetheart. Originally she was "Carmen Banana," but lawyers advised against imitating Miss Carmen Miranda so closely. We creative people felt that the change to Chiquita practically ruined the whole commercial, which shows how silly writers can get when their baby is kicked around.

Chiquita warned that "Bananas like the climate of the very very tropical equator, so never put bananas in the refrigerator."

Her calypso persuasion was so powerful that years after she went off the air, she came back to tell everyone about the way the company packed bananas in boxes where they were picked, instead of shipping them north on stems, thus avoiding bruises and other evils. Then we made a survey asking people what she said.

Guess what? "Never put bananas in the refrigerator!"

Like medicine and other sciences, banana science has forged ahead meanwhile, and it is now quite all right to put bananas in the refrigerator. But it seems unlikely that they will be put there until the generation who believed in the original Chiquita is gone.

Chiquita even had impact upon our management at the time. They gave each of the two men who wrote it a twenty-five-dollar Savings Bond in addition to their salary. Since the bonds cost $17.50 a piece, they were really tossing money about in a manner unheard of until then.

Many people object to singing commercials who could not tell how many days there are in April without going through a similar verse.

They will find it pleasant to learn that such commercials turn around occasionally and take a nip at agency people. There was once a gadget that, attached to the throat of an announcer, could mix recorded sounds with his voice. One such arrangement turned the announcer's voice into a foghorn which said, "Beeee-Ooooo" (for Body Odor).

One of our officers and his wife were amazed that this befogged B.O. was the first word their little darling ever spoke.

Radio's amazing vitality has continued in its old age. Ninety-eight per cent of homes have one or more radios, over 95 per cent have TV. Just for comparison, 88 per cent have telephones, which most of us would consider essential. And during the four years of television's greatest and most dramatic growth, 1948 through 1952, radio sets outsold TV sets two to one.

Radio continues to be an important medium (some say you can get more for your money on radio than anywhere else). And it will surely continue to be until science finds a way to combine TV with cars, stoves, irons and vacuum cleaners!

Stacy Page, a man who stuffed his own shirt, had a passingly pleasant voice that almost got him out of a mess of his own making. His client wanted to put on a one-shot radio show but he had only enough money for time, none for talent.

Don't worry! Stacy would think of something. What he thought of was Jimmy Durante, who never failed to help out at benefits. Jimmy agreed, but when he found out that *this* benefit was for a poverty-stricken client, he backed out.

There was nothing left for Stacy to do, but go on himself: It was reported that the client was not overjoyed. He was, in fact, underjoyed.

---

Two BBDOers visited Detroit during the 1935 World Series with Chicago. Detroit had gone crazy over its Tigers. Cut-outs of tigers were everywhere. One gas station had a huge banner: "BUY OUR GAS, IT'S TIGERIZED!" How close to fame that station man came!

# Iron lung
# with a view

## 25

☞ Television was never the child wonder that many thought it to be. It just had a long and troubled adolescence.

In 1923, only three years after the first radio broadcast, J. L. Baird in England and C. F. Jenkins in the United States demonstrated systems of mechanical television. In 1930 large-screen television was shown in England. In the same year BBDO forecast, "Television will assume a new importance for advertising." The prediction was right but somewhat like twenty years early.

It was held back mostly by the same old questions:

"Who is going to build cars until we get roads?"

"Who is going to telecast in color until people get enough color sets?"

"And who is even going to telecast anything until there are sets to view?"

On August 13, 1943, we began experimental television (*very* experimental!) by courtesy of General Electric over station WGRB, Schenectady. Anyone who cared to devote some of his time and talent to this unbelievable medium was invited to help. Art directors designed sets, copywriters concocted scripts, radio directors cast secretaries in dramatic parts and we put on some of the worst drama this side of summer stock.

This was called "getting your feet wet in television." Just why and how desirable that condition is, I do not know. But the boys and girls loved it. In nine months they put on twenty shows. The fan mail was not large, there were too few sets, but here and there an encouraging note came from people who preferred our dramas to diagonal lines, or even "snow."

After one particularly grueling telecast of *Miss Subways, 1943,* the whole beaten crew was standing on the railroad platform, dreaming of even greater triumphs to come.

Unfortunately, they were dreaming on the wrong platform and all climbed aboard the westbound express instead of the train to New York. Wherever they are, we are grateful to them. They pioneered with more exuberance than skill, they destroyed more vacuum tubes than they made sales but—by gad—they pioneered.

To quote from our own files of Dead Sea Scrolls: "As a result of their efforts, it is safe to say that no other agency has done or learned as much about Television. Our timing has been right. With interest in Television rising by advertisers, radio stations and motion picture companies, BBDO is on the beam."

Such huffing and puffing is okay for big executives, but we had an impatient art director named Chet Kuleza who believed that TV was already knocking on the door. Instead of playing with his paints and gazing out of the window, he galloped up and down the aisles shouting, "TV is Coming! TV is Coming!"

We appeased this noisy fellow by appointing a "TV Board" to keep its eye on this new thing. They did not have too long to wait. In 1949 we had a small TV department of about a dozen souls. By the end of the following year we had 150.

Some ink-stained writers and their contact counterparts openly resisted TV. Others moved with reluctant feet. But the majority of youngsters were wildly eager to get in.

Management, which by this time included me, made the age-old mistake of thinking that a new medium required a special kind

212

of writer. We wound up, as many other agencies did, with two copy departments—one for space, and one for radio-TV. These two creative groups naturally clashed. The youngsters who were flocking into writing for TV knew "MCU's," "Barn-door wipes," "Gobos" and all the pig latin of the new medium, but very little about advertising and sales basics. Indeed, I was told by one of the new breed that the program we were trying to sell was not the kind that could "be bastardized by commercials."

The radio-TV creative group delivered quite a few gift-wrapped packages with nothing in them. The space writers knew the ABC's of advertising and selling, all right . . . but they wanted to be transferred to where they could get some TV experience.

There was only one thing to be done. Amid resignations, wailings and protests we crunched the two departments into one under Bob Foreman.

The radio-TV writers were to learn (or re-learn) the techniques of writing for print. And the print writers, some of whom had never written one page of broadcast copy, were to get caught up on that skill. There was considerable blood on the ground. Both heads of the two former departments walked out. There were other resignations, some unaided, some aided. But it worked. And we avoided the day we all feared, when the client might receive one recommendation from the print writers and a different one from the TV writers.

We did, for a while, also have TV account executives—to work with those older men who couldn't or wouldn't learn TV. The TV account executive is also long gone. The diehards died or took themselves elsewhere.

One sacred cow that we all believed in was ground to hamburger. That was "sponsor identification." In radio the sponsor owned the show, and it was thought to be quite valuable if the talent got identified in the public mind with the product he was selling. When Jack Benny was on for Luckies, we wanted everyone to *associate* him with Lucky Strike, although many of his fans continued to associate him with J-E-L-L-O . . .

But whether "sponsor identification" is worth much or little, only the largest advertisers can afford it now. There are dual sponsorships, multiple sponsorships and a lot of non-sponsors who pop in around each station break.

In November 1956, Ben Duffy made a speech before the Television Sales Executives Club in which he decried the almost prohibitive costs of television.

"Four years ago [1952]," he said, "a half-hour network program cost in the neighborhood of $25,000, plus time cost . . . three years ago $30,000, last year around $39,000, and in the coming year it will be around $40,000. And an hour-long variety show that we considered had an initial budget of $150,000—for the program only, without considering time costs."

That was fifteen years ago.

Take a peek now!

That half-hour program that Ben watched grow from $25,000 to $40,000 over four years, costs today between $90,000 and $110,-000 (without time costs). An hour-long weekly program is in the area of $200,000.

An hour-long Special of the musical variety type can cost from $350,000 up—Bob Hope gets $450,000—Jacques Cousteau, $389,000.

And time costs are not exactly free. The average cost of a prime time hour on a network is now $185,000—a half-hour is $95,000.

More and more sponsors are buying on scatter plans—a commercial here, another there, on a variety of programs. *Goldfinger*, recently released, sold for $150,000 per commercial minute. Since the show has fourteen such minutes available, total cost (time and program) would be $1,100,000. The cost of a thirty-second announcement today is more than the entire Ann Sothern Show twenty years ago.

I tried to guess what the highest rating achieved by a single program had ever been. The answer is "The Bob Hope Show at Christmas 1970" which got 46 per cent of all TV homes, and "The Superbowl of January 1972," which reached 44.2 per cent of homes. How about the President? Well, he gets more than anybody because he takes all the networks. There is a small build of audience in local stations that are not carrying him.

With all these breathtaking costs few advertisers turn TV down, unless they have to. It can be seen in 66.1 million homes, which is over 95 per cent of all homes.

But how do you *know* how many people are viewing? Many

measurements have been tried, but I think that almost all agencies and clients now go by Nielsen. Nielsen has about 1,200 "audimeters" sitting in 1,200 family closets and recording every program that the TV set is tuned to, the number of minutes it is listened to, and even the portion of the program that drew the largest audience. A running tape records this information. When the cartridge of tape is filled, the cartridge pops out, is mailed to the Nielsen Organization, and a new tape put in.

To check the audimeter findings, Nielsen also has a separate group keeping a diary of their listening habits. It is pleasing to sponsors and agencies that the audimeters and the diaries check very well.

A friend of mine, Walter Tibbals, deceased like most of my better friends, once worked for a company that produces shows. One of the partners, who did not spend too much time in America, said:

"You will tell me pliz, about thees lettle machines that counts people who watch?"

"The Nielsen Audimeter!"

"Yes, how many of these machines?"

"About twelve hundred."

"And how many people in the United States?"

"Over two hundred million."

"So-o-o-o. Ees a lot of sheet, no?"

It is hard to believe that 1,200 people can be representative of all of us, but if they are a true sample, 1,200 is enough.

The audimeters are now being hooked directly to a computer —so the machines can report instantly to Big Brother and there will not be that business of waiting for people to mail in their tapes.

Anyone in the advertising business is constantly descended upon at cocktail parties by intellectual harpies who say, "I *never* watch television."

Sorry, lady, but a lot of people do. If you go to Toronto, notice the houses with high aerials all over town. That is what they use so they can get those lousy American programs instead of their own. If you go to Vero Beach, Florida, where they have to pay six dollars a month to get that nasty old TV—you'll find them getting up the six dollars from somewhere.

The number of hours in which the average person is at his TV set is:

| | |
|---|---|
| Men | 21 hours a week |
| Women | 28 hours a week |
| Teens | 19 hours per week |
| Children | 22 hours per week |

Of course, much of this watching is done together.

Many a heart, and many a pocketbook, has been broken by giving people what they *ought* to have instead of what they *want*.

When TV was new we used to produce our own shows at the agency, and buy an occasional one from a packager, or from the network itself. Now the network produces its own shows. It just happens, I guess, that their shows are always better than those put together outside—but when I remember how Smiling Jim Aubrey, head of CBS, literally kicked off the General Electric Show, in order to replace it with Judy Garland, I wonder.

The only fun left in TV is for the guys who put the commercials together, and they have more fun than anybody.

We were shooting a happy fisherman with a string of trout. Since we had no time to go fishing for trout (Sh-h-h-h), we bought them. Having found the perfect sylvan dell, we set up the cameras and looked for the fish. Nothing was found, but the wrapping that had been around the fish, and a dog with a big smile on his face! Fun!

Again we were shooting a chariot race on a beach . . . a real Ben Hur type of race. It is a sport we were trying to get started. But it never went over as a youth thing. One reason, perhaps, was that after several trial runs, and we were shooting for real, a horse dropped dead, and not even mouth-to-mouth resuscitation would bring him back.

Television brought the world (outside of the South) its chance actually to see that fine . . . that rich . . . that naturally mild tobacco.

It had to come from Richmond, where it sleeps.

It arrived about half an hour before air time and was as dry as crackle—click—pop.

At that very second one of advertising's unsung heroes grabbed the hand of tobacco and dashed out of the door yelling that he knew exactly what to do with it.

He grabbed a cab, dashed to the Luxor Baths, stripped and took the tobacco into the steam room.

Back he came with some moments left, but alas, the tobacco was as drippy as wet spinach.

"Don't worry—I know just what to do."

Instantly we all stopped worrying, of course.

Back he came again, and the tobacco was beautiful, fine, rich, naturally mild.

He'd had the "prop" woman *iron* it.

Our client who sponsored Burns and Allen had never been to Hollywood, and when contract renewal time came, he asked to go along. He was fascinated by the meeting but, as time elapsed, he became hungry and said so.

"Let's run over to my club, Hillcrest," Burns suggested.

"But isn't that a Jewish club?" our client asked.

"Sure," said George, "but I've got a brother who is a Jew. He can get us in."

---

TWX FROM LA

MET CLIENTS WIFE AS INSTRUCTED TOOK HER TO BEN BLUES RESTAURANT INTRODUCED HER TO BLUE STOP SHE SAID I DID NOT KNOW YOU WERE STILL AROUND STOP TOOK HER TO MEET HANDSOME JOHN FORSYTHE AT SHOOTING STOP SHE SAID MY GOD YOU LOOK JUST LIKE MY DEAD BROTHER STOP TOOK HER TO LAWRENCE WELK SHOW WE HAD LAWRENCE PRIMED TO MEET HER STOP WHEN WELK SAW US HE GAVE BATON TO SOMEONE ELSE AND ASKED CLIENTS WIFE SHALL WE DANCE QUESTION MARK SHE SAID CERTAINLY NOT EXCLAMATION POINT STOP PLEASE ADVISE

BUD

# What
# shall we say
# to the Africans?

---

## 26

☞ Years ago, a session of the House of Commons was interrupted by the exciting news that the cable to Africa had just been completed. After the hurrahing and hat tossing had died down, Winston Churchill rose and said, "Excellent! Splendid! Now what shall we say to the Africans?" England never did get the answer to that simple question, but advertising creative people must.

Creative effort before that simple question is answered is not only wasteful, but can get people even more confused than they are. Old-timers will tell you about the campaign warning against softened gums and headed: "Have You Got Pink Toothbrush?" Apparently most people didn't, because stores shortly sold out of pink toothbrushes. And the first "Kinsey Report" on the sex habits of the American male smartly increased the sale of Kinsey Whiskey.

Grinding out the answer to "What shall we say to the Africans?"

comes mighty close to nasty old thinking. And we do not need philosophers to tell us that "Men will bear almost any evil rather than go through the pain of thinking—of really thinking and thinking for themselves, then following through the results of their thinking."

The first thing to think about (and the last thing to forget) is that advertising is persuasion. Even a good lost dog ad offers some reward—some answer to the prospect's eternal question: "What's in it for me?"

In general Americans do not understand the uses of persuasion although individually they are masters of it. If an organization or a government or a political candidate makes use of persuasion, people are likely to brand it "propaganda"—a terribly bad word even though it was invented by Pope Julius for the College of Propaganda at the Vatican . . . a college devoted to the propagation of the faith.

In our efforts to win friends abroad (USIA and Voice of America), news is thought to be more desirable than persuasion, men put in charge are former newsmen, and nobody gets persuaded of anything much.

A woman who wished to quarrel with a talk I made said, "I hope to see the day when truth will take the place of persuasion." But this is nonsense. Persuasion and truth should go hand in hand, although they sometimes do not (see Dr. Goebbels and other Nazi purveyors of information).

When we look at our own lives, we feel quite different about persuasion. No kid ever got to take the family car because of the news that he was seventeen. No man ever won a bride reciting his vital statistics.

News tells us that a serum has been perfected that can protect us against polio, persuasion gets us to take the shots. News tells us that our alma mater is playing East Siwash next Saturday. Persuasion gets us to sit out in the rain. News tells us what women's styles are going to be. Persuasion gets them to wear the new styles. (In the case of the "midi" persuasion failed.)

News has a very important place in advertising, however. I believe I was the one who first said: "Put news in your product and it will put your product in the news." News is exciting, interrupting, attention-getting and curiosity-provoking. But unless your news is a basis for persuasion, it is just a lot of lovely noise.

Persuasion in advertising ought, they say, (a) to be truthful, (b) to be based on an *important* difference in the product and (c) to be based on an *exclusive* difference.

More important than any of these, it must link the product's most important benefit to the prospect's greatest need or strongest desire.

Do I dare sit here and say that advertising need not be truthful? I believe it must not mislead—but when it enters the field of fable and fantasy, it need not be true except in its product claims. Do you believe there really is a Jolly Green Giant?

And what about the important and exclusive difference?

It is because most products do not have all three advantages listed thus far that skillful creative people were born.

They have won believability where little existed, by TV demonstration, by the testimony of honest users, by guarantees and money-back offers. It has also been proven that belief in the company will strengthen belief in its products.

They have created importance where little existed, by stressing times and places where the product might have importance, and by getting the product associated with some important trend—such as "The Pepsi Generation."

A favorite advertising device of the past was to take a characteristic, common to many competitive products, and "make it yours" by stressing it oftenest and most. George Washington Hill, one of the all-time advertising greats, did this for Lucky Strike when he advertised "It's Toasted" a year or two before you were born. His competitors had the same process—but he named it and claimed it. But don't try it now—it's an FTC no-no.

Ben Duffy once told the FTC that advertisers wanted no more freedom than the average husband has when he tells his wife she is the most beautiful woman in the world. Scientifically, it is untrue. He knows it. She knows it. But everybody's happy. And no one is hurt.

If your product is unimportant enough, you can get away with this. No one believes that a stick of gum can "Double your fun." The claim is unimportant and non-exclusive—and even the FTC would hesitate to move against this merry little claim.

I do not think it wrong to sell a good product on its merits, without listing its demerits.

On the other hand, it must amaze you as it does me to see an advertiser destroy belief and importance in his wild grab for attention. Why should a perfectly good detergent have two fake Indians discussing the detergent's amazing ability to get smoke stains out of blankets? Why should a juvenile moron who apparently stuffs himself with sausages all day long sicken the air by his constant demand for more? Why should scruffy idiotic people of any kind profane their sponsor's products?

The reason, of course, is that between 500 and 1,000 advertising messages are thrown against each mind, each day. Somehow this "boredom barrier" must be broken through. The real trick, and the real trademark of a fine creative mind, is to find a way that gets attention—not only without destroying the message—but by actually enhancing it.

Commercials and print advertisements are as much in need of attractive packaging as any product. The two big money-wasters of today, I believe, are presenting the bare bones of a proposition with no packaging and presenting a beautiful gift-wrapped nothing. All beauty, no sell. Rosser Reeves estimates that more than half of all ads fall into the latter category. And how many times have you heard—indeed, said—"I saw the best commercial last night—I wish I could remember who the sponsor was!"

The first advertisement I ever wrote in an advertising agency was for Paniplus. If you never heard of it, the fault may have been mine.

Bakers have always had problems ever since someone sold them the idea that there were thirteen in a dozen. When I first became a card-carrying copywriter, their special problem was that they had switched from horses to trucks. One great service the horse had always done for the baker was to eat up all the "stales" that were returned from stores where they had lingered too long. Neither Chrysler, Ford nor General Motors had been able to come up with a truck that ran on stale bread.

Hence Paniplus. It was a hygroscopic agent, drew moisture from the air. Instead of getting stale, the bread got fresher and fresher until it puddled off the shelf onto the floor, I presume. For some reason, the bakers that made it wouldn't use it. They were probably planning a new advertising campaign: "Contains no Paniplus."

What a chance to be creative, to overwhelm my boss with the vastness of my skill! After a whole day, I had found nothing better than the first thing I wrote: "Cut Losses from Stales." I took it into the big man's window office rather reluctantly. John Caples had just convinced everyone that the best headlines began with "How to." So my boss changed the headline to: "How to Cut Losses from Stales." And that's the way it ran. No packaging. No picture. Just bare bones.

Today we would put it on TV (we wouldn't have the money, we're just playing pretend). A whole chorus of long-stemmed American Beauties would dance and sing: "Skip the bother! Skip the fuss! Just ask the man for Paniplus, with freshness it's loaded!"

Then one of those six-year-old geniuses, whose mother had drowned the wrong twin, would cut in, "Give us that name again, Sister." And the chorus would repeat, "Paniplus." We would then superimpose the name in a whole parade of leaping hieroglyphics, match dissolve to limbo, wipe to black, Roger and Over.

Naturally the PR department would have tipped off *Variety* and *Ad Age,* along with the principal newspaper ad columns. And the research boys would be there with freshly cut bench marks. The whole nation would have been made Paniplus conscious. The fact that nobody knew what Paniplus was—that we had left out all persuasion—might have even been forgiven by the client, who meanwhile had won enough Phony Awards to start his own hock shop.

The new techniques available to us today make the consideration of *how* we will say it a lot more interesting than *what* we will say.

For those left over from a past age—those who think the raw idea is enough—those who still believe in "Hard Sell" (shouted persuasion) are disappearing rapidly from the scene and it will not be long before we have Fast! Fast! FAST! relief from them.

What shall we say to the Africans?

How do we make sure that we have a message before we package it? The idea is not new, you know.

Horace, who is a bit older than any of us, wrote:

> *Sound judgement is the ground of writing well*
> *And when philosophy directs your choice*
> *To proper subjects rightly understood*
> *Words from your pen will naturally flow.*

And Bacon probably had the results of not doing so in mind when he wrote:

> This writing seemeth me not much better than the noise or sound which musicians make while they are tuning their instruments!

A proper understanding of the concept of first evolving the proposition—and then clothing it with beauty and excitement, might do away with the Big Meeting, too. Everyone in advertising has attended the Big Meeting. Everyone who can think and many who never tried are called in. The problem is explained. A date is set for a second Big Meeting. Everyone goes away and, naturally, everyone thinks in terms of his background and training. Back at the second Big Meeting comes a mad scramble of ideas, techniques, methods, pet projects and hopeful doodles that were well described by Carlyle, although he was trying to describe something else:

> It has no purpose, only purposes . . . wholly a vortex of vain councils, hallucinations, intrigues and imbecilities swirl like withered rubbish in the meeting of winds.

Just think, if the Big Meeting were limited only to finding the basic selling idea—with the packaging left 100 per cent to the creative people. There would be less Big Meetings. And creative people would spend more time making advertising and less time spinning their wheels.

For, as I have said before—good creative people are rare and valuable. And they are born, not made. I know that people have claimed that creative ability can be increased. I have no reason to doubt them. Yet even though it is true, I must be reminded of Dr. Johnson's remark upon hearing a female preacher for the first time:

> "Sir," he said, "it is like seeing a dog walk upon its hind legs. It is not well done, but the wonder is that it is done at all."

Letter found in an old man's outgoing basket

Once upon a time there came down from the Thessalian plain southward to the city of Athens a man dissatisfied. He entered the Agora and came upon Socrates.

"Sir," cried he, "I am a miserable fool!"

Socrates nodded.

"This thing is possible," he said.

"For here," went on the discontented one, "I have been striving these thirty years to build in Thessaly a Parthenon. And lo, I can manage only a mud hut!"

"Take heart, my friend," cried Socrates, "for you are in better case than most. For there are few enough men who try to build a Parthenon and, of the few, the most part build themselves a mud hut and take it for a Parthenon."

And the Thessalian went back to Thessaly and built his temple.

# Farewell
# to the troops

## 27

☞ Beside me as I write this is an application blank made to the Columbia University Summer Session in 1926.

Under their question of "Why, etc.?" I had answered, "I wish to pursue a career in advertising." I have indeed pursued it and occasionally damned near caught up with it.

The only thing I have found bad about advertising is that someday, if you don't get your coronary in time, you have to leave. In my case it will be at the end of this year.

It seems a bit ungracious just to creep away, without giving my friends a chance to ignore my advice. So here are some things I have learned in forty-three years:

1. Honesty is not only the best policy, it is rare enough today to make you pleasantly conspicuous.

2. The expedient thing and the right thing are seldom the same thing.

3. The best way to get credit is to try to give it away.

4. You cannot sink someone else's end of the boat and keep your own afloat.

5. If you get a kick out of your job, others will get a kick out of working for you.

6. It is not important that you come in early and work late. The important thing is *why?*

7. No one should knock research who has ever been helped by a road map.

8. Chicken Little acted before her research was complete. The competition ate her up.

9. A writer who can't take it had better win in the first round. Unfortunately very little advertising is okayed in the first round.

10. There has never been such a thing as a bad client, as long as he paid his bills.

11. A man of stature has no need of status.

12. Never trust a man who is Dr. Jekyll to those above him and Mr. Hyde to those under him.

13. There are fewer low-interest products than low-interest writers.

14. You learn more from your defeats than from your victories.

15. Few people are successful unless a lot of other people want them to be.

16. Many people know how to make a good living. Few know what to do with it when they have it made.

I have loved it here. I hope you do, too.

Charlie Brower